# ARTHUR BI

AND THE GLAS
LAKE VILI
1892 - 199

# ARTHUR BULLEID
## AND THE GLASTONBURY LAKE VILLAGE 1892 - 1992

By
JOHN COLES, ARMYNELL GOODALL
AND STEPHEN MINNITT

Somerset Levels Project and
Somerset County Council Museums Service
1992

*Published by the Somerset Levels Project and Somerset County Council Museums Service.*



***Reprinted 1993***

*ISBN 0 9507122 1 3*

*Design: Crispin Goodall Design Ltd*
*Printed by Short Run Press, Exeter*

Front cover: *reconstruction of Glastonbury Lake Village by M Forestier in 1910*
Back cover: *drawing of the Green Man by Arthur Bulleid.*

## Preface

In 1892, Arthur Bulleid discovered the Glastonbury Lake Village, now one of Europe's most famous archaeological sites. To commemorate the centenary of this event, we have compiled an account of the discovery and subsequent excavation of the Lake Village. Its story is inextricably linked with the life and work of Arthur Bulleid, who devoted 60 years to Lake Village and Somerset studies. We have also tried to incorporate aspects of the family life of Arthur Bulleid, of his long association with Harold St George Gray, and of his other interests and accomplishments.

The text has been written by John Coles (co-director of the Somerset Levels Project), Armynell Goodall (daughter of Arthur Bulleid) and Stephen Minnitt (Assistant County Museums Officer, Somerset County Museums Service). Certain personal passages of family history are written by Armynell Goodall and are generally designated by (AG) in the text. As Bulleid recorded measurements in the Imperial system this has been retained throughout the text.

We acknowledge the great assistance of the Somerset Record Office, the Glastonbury Antiquarian Society, the Somerset Local History Library, the Somerset County Museums Service and other sources of written and illutrative material. The book was designed by Crispin Goodall (Arthur Bulleid's grandson). We also thank Stephen Morland, John Loveridge, David Dawson, Carole Price, Susan Clements, Lawrence Bostock, Bob Croft, Bryony Coles, Hugh Chapman, Bruce Watkin, David Bromwich, Winifred Hutton, Charles Browne, Roy Minnitt, Adam Green and Peter Collings for encouragement and/or practical assistance.

The book has been published with financial aid from the Somerset Archaeological and Natural History Society, the Glastonbury Antiquarian Society, the Somerset County Council Museums Service and Environment Department, the Somerset Levels Project and the Maltwood Fund for Archaeological Research in Somerset. We are grateful for this support.

1. *Bulleid brothers Lawrence, Howard and Arthur*

## Early Days

Arthur Bulleid was born in Glastonbury in 1862, the youngest child of J G L Bulleid and his wife Christiana (née Wooff). J G L Bulleid was a solicitor and a prominent citizen of Glastonbury, where he was mayor no less than seven times. He had a strong interest in antiquarian matters, and was founder (1886) and first President of the Glastonbury Antiquarian Society. Arthur and his two brothers Howard and Lawrence were educated at St John's College, Hurstpierpoint, commonly known as 'Hurst'. Founded by Nathaniel Woodard, an Anglican clergyman with High Church leanings, the school catered for 'middle class boys' with a wide curriculum; this was in contrast to many public schools where Classics predominated. The fees at Hurst were £20 a year.

> 'My father was not happy at school; he said the boys were half starved during Lent and during the winter they were cold. He won a prize for drawing, he was a prefect in his last year (1879), played football for the First XI and obtained his Swimming Certificate, and finally he was the Chamberlain in a production of Henry IV part I'. (AG)

Perhaps Bulleid had been conditioned to the cold of school by his adventures as a very small boy. When he was 4, he was found one cold winter's day walking purposefully along Magdalene Street in Glastonbury; an elderly gentleman said to him, 'Well young Bulleid where are you going?' He replied 'I am going to test the ice'.

After leaving Hurst, Bulleid went to the Potteries to learn the trade as an apprentice, returning to Glastonbury to work with patterns and glazes in a local company. He found little to encourage him in his efforts to experiment and develop the craft, and he abandoned the work and turned to medicine. He entered the Bristol Medical School from where he could visit his parents in Glastonbury whenever possible. Bulleid had a slight hesitation in his speech which worried him all through his life and he found oral examinations difficult. Nonetheless his career as a doctor seemed assured and he pursued his studies vigorously. Yet there was always another interest, instilled by his father, in antiquarian matters, and in his spare time he read of the excavations and discoveries then being made in Britain and abroad.

## The discovery of the Glastonbury Lake Village

In the winter of 1853-54, some dredging took place in the harbour of a small lakeside town, Meilen, in Switzerland. A vast array of wooden piles, antler and stone tools were brought up and thus began a great episode of 'lake-dwelling' research in Switzerland, France and Italy. After some years, a detailed yet popular book was prepared by Ferdinand Keller, President of the Antiquarian Society of Zurich, and an English edition appeared in 1878, called *The Lake Dwellings of Switzerland and Other Parts of Europe*. Bulleid, his own antiquarian interests already strong, and living beside a wetland, read the book and considered that the Somerset moors and swamps might well hold traces of ancient settlement like those of the Swiss lakes. He wrote about his search:

> 'For four years as opportunities occurred, the moorlands were explored looking for probable sites, more particularly in the peat-cutting localities of the Shapwick and Edington Burtle Turbaries. On a Wednesday afternoon in March, 1892, when driving across the moor from Glastonbury to Godney, a field was noticed to be covered with small mounds, an unusual feature in a neighbourhood where the conformation of the land is for miles at a dead level. On the following Sunday afternoon the field was visited, and anticipations were agreeably realized by picking up from the numerous mole-hills a number of pottery fragments, a whetstone, and pieces of bone and charcoal. The same evening in course of conversation a valued friend and neighbour, Mr EDWARD BATH, became interested in the matter, and having intimated that he believed the field belonged to him, a note arrived the following morning to confirm this, with permission to dig, subject to making arrangements with the tenant. This was done, and a week or two later tentative excavations took place by digging trenches into two of the mounds. The sections exposed clay floors with hearths, supported by massive timber substructures. Quantities of pottery, bones of animals, several implements of bone and antler, and a beautifully polished jet ring or bead, were among the relics discovered during these preliminary investigations. As the water level was still high and flooded the trenches, it

> was deemed advisable to postpone the exploration until the summer. In the meantime the matter was brought before the Glastonbury Antiquarian Society, and a fund was started with the object of making a systematic examination of the site, and Mr EDWARD BATH generously made a gift of five acres of land (including the site of the village) to the Glastonbury Antiquarian Society. Investigations were begun towards the end of July 1892'.

Bulleid wrote a short report on his discoveries to a London newspaper, addressing his letter to 'The Editor, Athenaeum', but no notice was taken of it. He also wrote to Lt General Pitt Rivers, then considered to be the leading expert on archaeological excavations in Britain, describing the mounded fields and the objects recovered from the first trench. Pitt Rivers seems to have misunderstood the nature of the site, thinking it to be a series of burial mounds, but his reply was nonetheless useful to the young Bulleid:

> July 4 1892
>
> 'The tumuli you speak of appear to be of interest owing to the deposits in them. I suppose you are keeping all the bones with a view to them being measured for estimating the stature of the people a point of considerable interest. And the fragments of pottery should of course be kept so as to compare them with other finds of the same description. Plans and sections of the tumuli would also be valuable ...'.

## The First Excavations 1892

In late July 1892 Bulleid set out the first trenches of his campaign at the Glastonbury Lake Village, uncovering the remains of clay floors, hearths and wooden beams, and recovering a large number of artefacts of stone, metal, pottery, glass, shale and wood. He had already formulated plans for a major, perhaps total, excavation of the village. Little did he know the problems of site and personalities that he would encounter, nor the friends he would make and supporters who would come forward to help him. John Morland, one of the father figures of Somerset archaeology, 'adopted' Bulleid's cause and, in early September 1892,

wrote a letter to Robert Munro, a Scottish doctor who had recently published a large volume on *The Lake Dwellings of Europe*, and who was probably the antiquary most experienced in such matters; Munro had just completed a tour of most of the European lakeside and crannog settlements. He made the journey down to Bristol and thence to Glastonbury on September 20th,

2. *Timber foundations and parallel logs representing collapsed palisade at the southern end of Glastonbury Lake Village*

> 'and in the evening met Messrs Morland and Bulleid, who kindly showed me the relics already collected and preserved, partly at Mr Bulleid's residence, and partly in the local Museum. I was astounded at the number and variety of the objects, many of which were unmistakably ornamented with Late-Celtic designs. Next morning we visited the site of the discovery, and on approaching a mass of upturned soil in a low-lying grassy field, which my companions pointed out as the digging, I almost involuntarily exclaimed, 'But where are the mounds you speak of?' 'There they are; we are just walking over them.' It was only then that I

noticed some slight elevations amidst the long grass with which the meadow was covered. Mr Bulleid explained that when the grass was short these mounds were more conspicuous than at present, as the more luxuriant vegetation in the hollows tended to mask the undulating surface of the field.

On stepping into the nearest trench we were confronted with a well displayed section of one of the mounds showing three oak beams lying over a bed of decayed brushwood, evidently *in situ*. Each of these beams contained two or three mortised holes, and through each hole the top of an upright pile protruded.'

Munro was convinced of the importance of the discovery and began a campaign which in retrospect can be seen as having two aims:

1. to help Bulleid as excavator and young British archaeologist.
2. to ensure that he, Munro, would come to be identified as the great interpreter of the site.

He wrote to Bulleid in early October:

'I am writing a short sketch of my visit to your locality which if I can get inserted into an influential journal I will publish. .... small scribblings in local journals do little good. I shall be glad to hear how you progress, but I presume little more can be done this season and you have time to make arrangements for next summer. A little attention to the excellent work already done and the importance of the discovery from high quarters would do your committee good - and these are points I keep in view in my notice. But say little about this until you see it in print'.

Munro's 'notice' took up a large part of a page in *The Times* and provided an account of the discovery of the Lake Village and a description of the structures and finds, prefaced by an essay on humanity. It began:

'One of the distinguishing characteristics of civilized man is an intense desire to become acquainted with the phenomena of his environment, and among the various departments into which his accumulated knowledge falls to be classified there is none more fascinating than that which deals with the original early history of his own race.'

The result of this exposition was a flood of reports in other newspapers, some based only upon Munro's notice, others more energetically based on visits to Somerset. Only two need be quoted here, as they took rather different approaches to the subject of archaeology, the remote past, and the Somerset moors:

'Over the wide expanse of turf moor hangs the haze of an autumn morning. The low hills are so veiled in mist that the vast plain, whose level is interrupted only by the embankments of the slow moving moorland rivers, seems to melt away into measureless distance. Quiet streams they are today; and yet a year ago these low lying lands were covered far and wide by their tawny flood'. *(Daily News)*

'The most industrious archaeologists and anthropologists have had to confess times without number how utterly they have been baffled in their attempts to fill in the gaps by which they are confronted in tracing the history of man from the earliest times. Many elaborate theories, built on almost a pin-point of conjecture, have been shattered by the unearthing of some tiny relic, the possible existence of which had perhaps never entered into the calculations of the Scientists.'*(Bristol Daily Post)*

Each of these reports eventually comes to the subject of the Lake Village and Arthur Bulleid. Locally, the discoveries excited much interest, much confusion it has to be said, and some ammunition for local commentators. *Jan an' Betty* were two of these, appearing in verse from time to time in the newspaper, and seemingly housing within their imaginary characters something of the emotion of those who lived and worked in the moors.

*Jan's Thauts 'Bout Th' Burtish Vullige*

'Down in moor th' de zay
That lately tha've a voun'

Al'zorts, boans be th' scoor,
Vaur veet unner groun'.

Boans a' hosses, boans a' zheep,
Boans a' deers, an' cow boans too,
Taup wun nuther al' o' a heap,
'Zif th'ud a gro'd thur zoo.

An' a vullige wur thur, th' de zay,
Back in th' wulden time,
'Tis gro'd al'auver wi gras,
An' now thur's skearce a zine."

There are 21 verses, but these three are probably enough for anyone.

## The Excavation Committees

Matters were more than local, however, and Bulleid found himself the recipient of advice from all quarters, invitations to speak to antiquarian societies, and at the centre of efforts made to establish a secure base for the excavations. The Glastonbury Antiquarian Society set up a committee to administer the work, to acquire funds, and to ensure local support. Furthermore, steps were taken to assemble a Committee of Reference and Advice, and all the heavy-weights were persuaded to join:

J G Baker, Esq, FRS, FLS
Professor Boyd Dawkins, FRS, FSA
Sir John Evans, KCB, FRS, FSA
The Right Hon Sir Edward Fry, FRS, FSA
Dr R Munro, FSA Scot
Lieut-General Pitt-Rivers, FRS, FSA

There was an appeal for funds and the response was good. Pitt Rivers wrote to Bulleid in spring 1893, enclosing a cheque for £5 and, more importantly, responding to news of the site:

> 'The photographs appear to be very good. My experience of over 20 years as an excavator has led me to think it of great importance to preserve, tabulate and classify *every* fragment of pottery found and to note

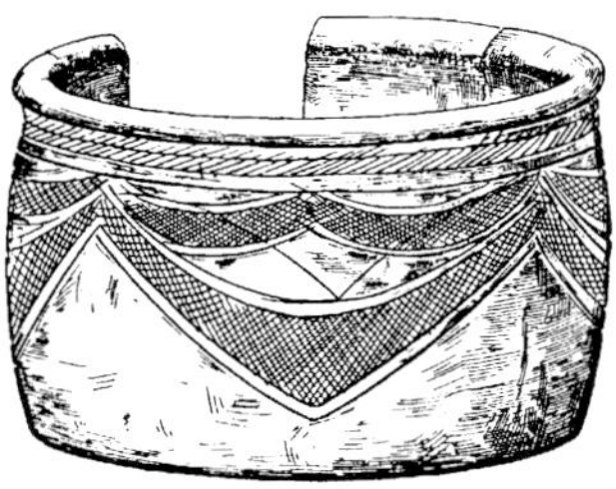

the depth. Pottery is in many cases the only reliable evidence of date attainable, and it is so persistent in its form and quality that the percentage of fragments of different kinds generally leads to important results ...'

This advice was sound and was followed by Bulleid insofar as it was possible, although the quantities sometimes overwhelmed him and his small team.

These developments all took place within a very few months of the discovery, before any real programme of excavation had been devised, and Bulleid must have been bewildered by it all. His medical studies were approaching a stage where only an oral examination was required for qualification. At his first attempt he was unsuccessful, and he decided to abandon medicine and become a full-time archaeologist, unsalaried and reliant upon his parents for his continued well-being.

Late in 1892 Bulleid received an invitation to lecture in London, at the Society of Antiquaries in Burlington House. This was the premier society and he asked Munro for

3. *Pottery drawings by Arthur Bulleid for publication in the first volume of the Glastonbury excavation report*

advice. Munro had other plans, as he was President-elect of the British Association, due to meet in Nottingham in 1893, and he wanted the Lake Village unveiled there. He wrote:

> '.. By all means go to London and give the Society of Antiquaries the benefit of your discoveries. I would however advise you to adhere to a description of actual facts and don't be enticed into the pitfall of explaining everything... Such a report if revised by your scientific experts would be a most valuable record. From this point of view you should not let all the details leak out into too many channels..'

and again:

> 'I have no doubt your paper will be highly appreciated at Burlington House and, if you avoid the rock on which young archaeologists generally come to grief, I have no doubt it will be a great success. The dangerous rock is to attempt to explain everything. The words late Celtic, pre and post-Roman Gauls or Britons or Saxons should not once appear in your paper. Describe exactly what you found, where found and in what circumstances, and you will start a firm basis. Keep all your speculations for the British Association. There you can indulge in conjectures and theories as much as you please.'

Bulleid's lecture to the Society was a success although we do not know if he refrained from conjecture - probably he did, and this may have been the starting of the very real emphasis, in all his reports, upon the observations made and recorded, upon the artefacts found, and upon the structures and deposits seen, measured and drawn. It has an obvious advantage for us today; we can believe what Bulleid says he saw, because he was so careful in his recording. Sir Harry Godwin, writing of his own acquaintance with Bulleid in the 1930s, said that Bulleid was 'a man of strongly scientific bent with decided geological as well as archaeological interest', and all of Godwin's scientific work on peat and pollen analysis confirmed Bulleid's views about the environmental conditions of the Lake Village. Of course, there is a disadvantage in Bulleid's reluctance to interpret beyond what he could record; it would be fascinating to know what he thought about some of the problems we will mention later.

## The British Association Lecture 1893

The meeting at Nottingham in 1893 was a great success, by all accounts. Munro as President was in his element, and introduced Bulleid to a large and appreciative audience. But he had been warned off anything but the bare facts once again, Munro having asserted beforehand that as Professor Boyd Dawkins was to follow Bulleid's paper, 'this will relieve you of all speculations'. Nonetheless, it was Bulleid's chance to set out the latest results of his work, and to present some views on the Lake Village now that he had examined a number of mounds. His opinions were not to vary much thereafter on the structure of the settlement, although vast quantities of finds were still to come, the palisade to trace, and many mounds to explore. In 1893 the most sensational find had already come to light (although Bulleid was not to know it was 'the best'). This was a bronze bowl, decorated by domed rivets, and repaired in antiquity; it was found outside the palisade. Eventually it came to be the motif of the Lake Village and to appear on the cover of the monographs. The Glastonbury Bowl, as it was called, has sometimes been confusingly attached to the Abbey (the sacred cup etc) and many replicas were made for sale to visitors to the town. In 1909 the Church of England final-

4. *The Glastonbury Bowl, drawn by Arthur Bulleid*

ly came into possession of the Abbey ruins, and to celebrate this great event the Prince and Princess of Wales, the Archbishop of Canterbury and other dignitaries descended upon the town and processed in stately fashion to the ruins, in the rain. The Glastonbury Antiquarian Society, owner of the Bowl, had a silver replica made to present to the Prince and Princess - alas, a jeweller of Glastonbury had already made and presented a Bowl to the royal couple.

Bulleid's paper to the British Association was well-received, and was summarized in *The Times*. In part it read:

> 'There is little on the surface to indicate the site of a village, but on careful inspection between 60 and 70 low circular mounds may be seen, varying from 15 to 35 feet in diameter, and from 6 inches to 2ft 6in high at the centre. These form the foundations or floors of separate dwellings, which are constructed in the following way:- On the surface of the peat is a layer or platform of timber and brushwood kept in place by numerous small piles at the margin. On this a layer of clay is placed, slightly raised at the centre, where the remains of a hearth are generally found. The dwelling itself was composed of timber filled in with wattle and daub. Not only have the wall-posts been found *in situ*, but also the entrance threshold and doorstep. The extent of the ground covered by the 60 or 70 mounds measures more than 400 feet north and south, by 300 feet east and west. The east border of the settlement has been met with, and is well defined by a thick line of piles and timber. This side of the village was undoubtedly, to begin with, protected by water, which in course of time was replaced by an accumulation of a peaty nature. It is in and on this formation outside the settlement that many interesting structures entering into the construction of the village have been unearthed, such as banks of clay and stone, morticed timber and hurdlework. Among other things that have been discovered is a boat 17 feet long, quantities of wheel and hand-made pottery, sling stones, and bones of animals, and great number of objects of bronze and iron, horn, bone and stone, such as fibulæ and rings, knives, saws, and weapons, combs, needles, pottery stamps and querns ...
>
> Whatever might be the ultimate conclusion arrived at

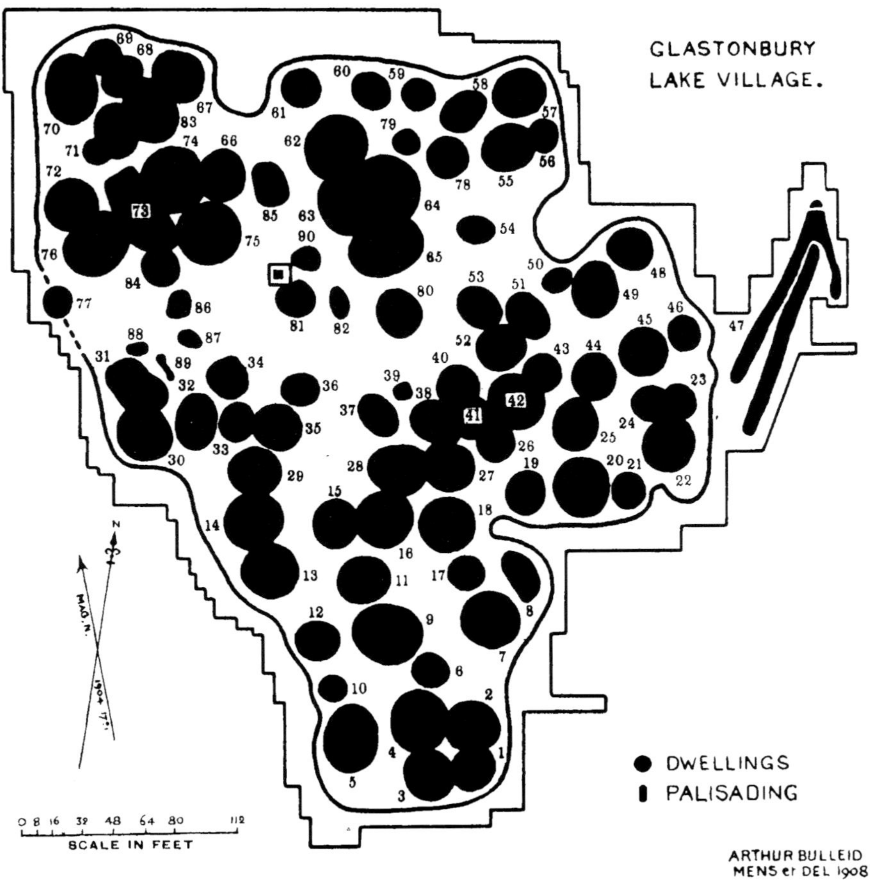


*5. Plan of Glastonbury Lake Village showing the positions of the 90 mounds, the causeway and the line of the surrounding palisade*

as to the probable date of the village, and who the occupants of these dwellings might have been, they had already gained some considerable amount of knowledge of the life they lived, the discoveries proving them to have been skilful workers in metals and carpentry, and also manufacturers of pottery. They also knew that they were basket makers, and acquainted with the lathe. It was obvious also from the wheat and beans, the bones of sheep and cattle, that they had tilled and farmed the adjoining highlands, and that they used the horse and dog, and lastly they were makers of fabrics, the texture of which, in some cases, they could not do otherwise than assume was in harmony with the fine and delicate fibulæ used for fastening them."

Following the factual account, Boyd Dawkins attempted an assessment of the results but his lecture seems to have consisted mostly of anecdotes, including the novel idea that the weavers of Glastonbury had probably used their antler combs not only in weaving but had also learned

> 'that it was a pleasant thing with which to scratch the head and comb the hair, and from this discovery the comb gradually grew and developed until it reached that elaborate ornament with which we are so familiar'.

Boyd Dawkins also thought that the Lake Dwellers could manage horses, could smelt bronze, and had indulged in cock-fighting.

The major achievement of this widely-reported meeting, and Bulleid's lecture, was that the public began to appreciate that 'these old Belgic inhabitants of Somerset were not the wild savages we have been accustomed to think them'. The everyday character of the finds, the broken pottery, animal bone, the wooden tools, and the personal ornaments, all could be identified as 'human' in the sense of the common artefacts of life; in the late 19th century it was just these things and these materials that surrounded the ordinary man and woman in their daily lives. The Museum in Glastonbury, established only 6 years before, was regularly thronged with people, especially on the free evenings.

## Subscribers and Entertainments

The Glastonbury Antiquarian Society was responsible for the excavations, and had now to raise sufficient funds for the work. Bulleid signified his willingness to work virtually full-time at no salary, but labourers and materials had to be paid for, and a campaign was mounted to find subscribers who could support the work. The excavation accounts for the first three years show that the subscriptions yielded £186-2-9, with entrance fees to the excavation field totalling £30-14-6. The expenses were as follows:

6. *Bulleid in the doorway of the Glastonbury Lake Village excavations site hut*

| | |
|---|---|
| Labour | £141-4-1 |
| Shed, Railing | £12-7-11 |
| Tools etc | £15-2-5 |
| Work on the boat | £1-15-0 |
| Photographs | £4-0-5 |
| Office expenses | £11-15-1 |
| A Bulleid expenses | £10-10-0 |
| Incidental expenses | £3-2-6 |

This left a balance of £15-17-7.

The Antiquarian Society occasionally held 'entertainments' in order to raise funds, and these generally gained large and appreciative audiences. One such entertainment had the following programme:

Polka March, *En Revenant de la Reine*, Glastonbury Orchestral Society
Song, *Hybrias the Cretan*, Rev G Beilby
Pianoforte Solo, *The Gypsy Ronde*, Miss Gaston
Recitation, Mr J A Bright
Song, *The Outpost*, Mr Davis
Lancers, *Olivette,* Glastonbury Orchestral Society
Song, Mrs R J Haine
Paper, *The Abbey under the first Norman Abbot*, Mr G W Wright
Duet (violin and pianoforte), Mr and Miss Davis
Reading, Rev G Beilby
Pianoforte solo, *Faust,* Miss Gaston
Song, *Coming through the rye*, Mrs R J Haine
Reading, *The Baron of St Castine*, Rev W E Francis
Galop, *John Peel*, Glastonbury Orchestral Society
*God Save the Queen*

This event may have finished after midnight as Mr G W Wright was an enthusiastic speaker who did not often overlook any detail in his subject.

During the first three years there were many visitors to the Museum and to the excavations. Parties came from all over the country, mostly Antiquarian, Naturalists', and Field Clubs and Societies. One such visit as reported in the press in September 1892, brought the Bath Field Club who arrived by the Somerset and Dorset Railway (now long gone) at Glastonbury. 'The club is one of those excellent societies formed with a view of promoting a taste among its members for scientific and archaeological inquiry, and this, more particularly, by combining with their intellectual researches visits to localities of general interest to the tourist'. The party, numbering 30, were met by Lawrence Bulleid (brother of Arthur) and conveyed to the Museum; from there the members went to the residence of J G L Bulleid where most of the Lake Village relics were stored. 'Here in a shed reposes the ancient boat, which after a submersion, of probably 2000 years in the boggy substratum at Cranhill Farm, has at last, been brought to light, in its entirety, and, to the eye at least, exhibiting signs of present strength ...' From here the party walked the 1.5 miles to the Lake Village excavations (only 200-300 yards from Cranhill Farm) where Arthur Bulleid described and demonstrated the work and discoveries. The Clifton Antiquarian Club came by train from Bristol to Wells, and thence by char-a-banc to the site, and the North Staffordshire Naturalists' Club and Cardiff Naturalists' Society were also accommodated by the Bulleid family in these very early days.

*7. Arrangements for one of the many group visits to the Glastonbury excavations*

*8. Drawing by Bulleid of timber at the edge of an unspecified clay floor at Glastonbury Lake Village*

# Wincanton Field Club.

## The LAST EXCURSION of the SEASON

IS FIXED FOR

MONDAY, SEPTEMBER 25TH, 1893.

*In accordance with a vote taken at the Annual Meeting, the Committee have decided to visit the*

## GODNEY LAKE DWELLINGS

*on the date above given.*

☞ It is decided to go by the train leaving Wincanton at **9-43,** and to return from Glastonbury by the train leaving **5-58.**

**TICKETS, including Railway fare, Admission to Museum, Grounds of Lake Dwelling, and Tea, 3/6 each.**

*No arrangement will be made for anyone not applying by Monday, the 18th instant.*

*GEORGE SWEETMAN, Secretary.*

*Wincanton, Sep.* 5, 1893,

Amor, Printer, Wincanton.

9. *A well preserved section of wicker work, possibly collapsed walling, found beneath mound 56 at the Glastonbury settlement*

## Excavations, analyses and illustrations

Bulleid's examination of the Lake Village had been planned from the start to expose the entire site, all of the mounds and palisade; the area to be excavated was 130 x 100 yards, and the depth of deposits could extend to 6 feet. In the first phase of excavation, 1892 to 1898, Bulleid worked to an open plan, uncovering wide areas mound by mound, and exploring long stretches of the palisade.

Photographs of the site show entire house platforms exposed. He had a small team of professional labourers who soon developed the ability to excavate carefully and rapidly, leaving delicate woodwork to be fully exposed by Bulleid himself. In 1894, for example, in an excavation lasting five months, nine mounds were explored but the major thrust of the work was concentrated on the border palisading of the Village where fully 400 feet was exposed in a series of trenches and wider areas. At the same time, the peat outside the palisade was exposed, revealing quantities of debris discarded from the settlement. Operations here had to be discontinued due to the high water table, even in late summer, as the pumps, in continuous use, could not cope with the flooding. Part of another wooden boat, 20 feet long, was found as well as finely-carved and decorated wooden objects, pottery, bone and metalwork. Most of this material went into the temporary storerooms at J G L Bulleid's home; by the end of the 1896 season he, the father, reported to the Society that the Glastonbury Museum must obtain more space as four of the rooms in his own home were now filled to overflowing.

Arthur Bulleid had had enough training in science, before he began to excavate, to realize that he alone could not hope to understand all the deposits of the Lake Village (peat, leaves, seeds, wood) or all of the finds (pieces of iron, bronze, stone and bone). He was very much a beginner in archaeology and he was quick to ask for and receive guidance from his Committee of Reference and Advice, among whom were Dr Munro and Professor Boyd Dawkins. These two were the principal advisers, and, with their encouragement, Bulleid was put in contact with a number of specialists. C W Andrews of the Natural History Museum agreed to look at the bird bones from the Lake Village, Boyd Dawkins of the Manchester Museum seized the human remains for analysis and comment, J G Baker of Kew (one of the Committee) advised on peat and seeds, and was succeeded by Clement Reid who also worked on the cereals, wheat cakes and plum stones; H E Balch, then working in the caves of the Mendips, came in at a later date to discuss the geology of the surrounding area, and Charles Read of the British Museum sent advice on the draughtsmanship that would be required when the report on the work was to be published; he visited the site and the Museum, and wrote 'my own opinion is that your diggings are more interesting and of greater archaeological importance than anything done for years'. This was high praise indeed and coming so soon (1894) into the work must have encouraged Bulleid in his project.

Read was the principal influence on Bulleid's style of drawing. Already an artist of some experience, Bulleid's pencil drawings of the decorated pottery were exquisitely executed, but Read said that pencilwork was no good for publication and a pen and 'very black ink' were needed to produce firm lines for shading. Bulleid accepted this advice and all his drawings of pottery are characterised by the firmness of line and density of shading; they are exceptionally

10. *Bulleid's finest pottery drawings were executed in pencil*

well-done yet the original drawings of the pottery done with a soft pencil really have to be seen in order to appreciate them for what they are – works of art.

Bulleid also drew the wooden artefacts before they entered into that limbo that is neither freshly-exposed nor fully-conserved, and he took the decision to draw the objects as originally conceived, smoothly uniform bowls, axle-boxes, laths from a frame, or mallets. The wood, although

11. *Worked timber photographed by Bulleid and interpreted by him as 'parts of looms or appliances for making textile fabric'*

appearing to be as firm as new wood, had the consistency of soft cheese and upon exposure to sun and wind it rapidly shrank, twisted and cracked. Bulleid was concerned about conservation of the smaller worked pieces, and could not hope to save the larger beams and piles. He sought advice from various quarters. Pitt Rivers sent a rather unintelligible letter suggesting 'metallated' (methylated?) spirits and gelatine, but commented that the Lake Village beams if so treated would require long troughs and 'a good deal of stuff'. Charles Read preferred silicate of soda, painted on while the objects were still wet.

## Election to the Society of Antiquaries of London 1895-96

Only three years after discovering the Lake Village, Bulleid was being considered for election to the Society of Antiquaries of London. Charles Read was Secretary of the Society, the most ancient antiquarian society of Britain, and in 1895 he offered to make the formal proposal himself, on the traditional Blue Paper which is still used by the Society; by December 12th 1895 the paper of candidature was on its way. The procedure was that the name was proposed to Council and, if agreed, was thereafter presented to the whole Fellowship which formed the electorate. Candidates could be, and sometimes were, blackballed. Bulleid's Blue Paper lies in the Society's archive and is transcribed here, by courtesy of the Society.

---

*Name.* Arthur Bulleid
*Addition, Profession or Occupations.* Student of Medicine
*Residence.* Glastonbury
*Qualification.* Attachment to the study of Antiquities; exploration of Late Celtic Village, Glastonbury
*being desirous of admission into the Society of Antiquaries of London, We, the undersigned, recommend him as likely to become a useful and valuable Fellow thereof.*
*Dated* this 6 day of December 1895.
(Signed by Fellows)

| *Personal Knowledge* | *General Knowledge* |
|---|---|
| A Wollaston Franks P(resident) | A Pitt Rivers |
| Charles H Read Sec | |
| Francis L Griffith | |
| John Evans V-P | |

Arthur J Evans
F G Hilton Price Dir(ector)
R Milburn Blakiston
*Proposed* December 12 1895
*To be balloted for* June 4 1896

---

What was exceptional about this Blue Paper was that Bulleid had barely begun his archaeological career, and that his list of signatories contained the names of virtually all of the leading figures of the day, the President, Secretary and Director of the Society, the two Evans and Lt General Pitt Rivers. Although the ballot itself is confidential, no one would dare to try to blackball such a candidate with that list of supporters.

In the same year (1895), Bulleid heard about another site:

> 'The late Mr STEPHEN LAVER, who lived and farmed land at Westhay, a hamlet in the parish of Meare, had seen on several occasions specimens from the Lake-Village exhibited at the Glastonbury Museum. On a Monday in September, 1895, he left a small parcel at my father's office, with a note, saying, 'Found when digging post-holes for the rails round a hay stack.' The parcel contained, to my surprise and pleasure, an ornamented fragment of Pre-historic Iron Age pottery, a stone spindle-whorl, and a whetstone ... Realizing that a farmer who rented land liable to flooding would place his hay stack on a mound or raised piece of ground, it was only necessary therefore when searching for the site to examine the hay-stacks in the locality of Westhay and Meare. This was done systematically, and on the third Sunday's walk the site was discovered. Not only was the site found, but from the side of a ditch which happened to cut through the margin of one of the dwelling-mounds, fragments of a large pot were protruding.'

As the work at the Glastonbury Lake Village was all-consuming of time, Bulleid decided to leave the site at Meare for the future. There was no way he could have dug at Meare – he was full-time at Glastonbury, working for 6 months on-site and 6 months on the materials and records. The excavations started at 7 am and ended at 6 pm, but Bulleid said he was often on site at 5 am and rarely left the field until 8 pm.

## Publicity

As work went on, the interest of the press remained high, parties continued to visit and popular lectures were given by Bulleid, by John Morland (an indefatigable supporter) and by Professor Boyd Dawkins who clearly was enjoying *his* role, in spite of Munro, as the great interpreter of the site and its place in British prehistory. Those entrusted with the task of making reports on the lectures in national and local newspapers did not hesitate to elaborate on the scholarly lectures. An enterprising reporter for the *Central Somerset Gazette* produced an annotated list of the discoveries, ending with

> '... a large block of oak, with pivots at both ends, evidently intended for a door, but whether for the front door (which seems improbable, as no knocker is attached), the aperture which served as a window to the ancestral mansion, or for a sluice, Mr Bulleid would not as yet venture to say. A piece of bread, baked in the form of a bun, and about the same size, has also been turned up. The baker, it is evident, was a few centuries in advance with the Allinsonian wholemeal theory, and in fact this specimen at any rate shows that no very careful use was made of the handsome mill querns found some time since, for the grains of wheat appear in the bread quite unbroken. However, this 'find' can scarcely be regarded as a fair specimen, for it is so manifestly overbaked, that no doubt it was cast aside on that account. A quantity of broken crockery and other fragments, near by, may or may not have some connection with a worthy warrior's wrathful reception of his spoiled meal.'

Nor was Boyd Dawkins reticent about conjecture, announcing that the Lake Village inhabitants had invented the safety-pin, the *County Gazette* noting that its evolution should 'afford a theme sufficiently absorbing for the newest New Woman capable of appreciating the relation of mechanical contrivances to human comfort'. But even Boyd Dawkins 'was unable to furnish any primeval clue to the peculiarities of pronunciation which prevail in that county' of Somerset; the *Western Gazette* could not 'refrain from reflecting what far wider deductions might have been drawn from the materials available, by the late lamented Mr S Holmes'.

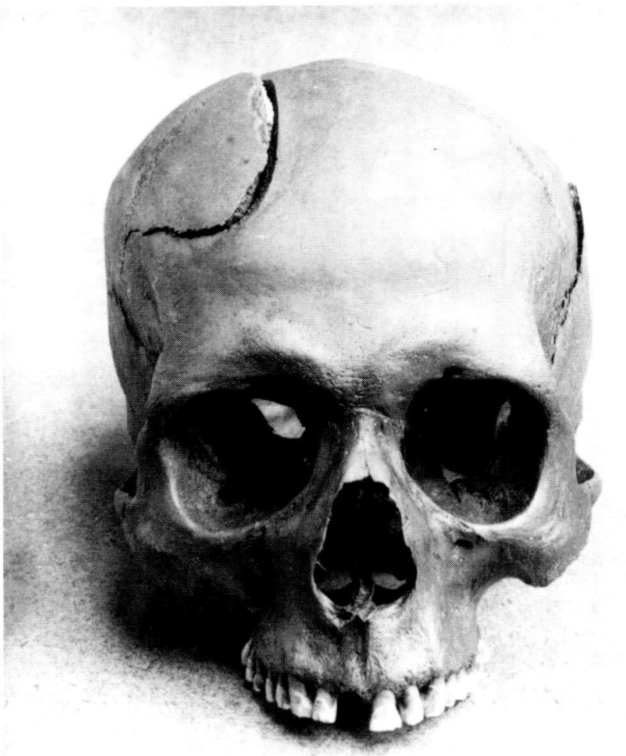

12. *Human skull from Glastonbury bearing a sword cut and believed by Boyd Dawkins to be evidence of a massacre*

Where Bulleid departed from his scientific and much more famous advisers was over the question of the human remains found in the Lake Village deposits. Boyd Dawkins as early as 1896 had interpreted the rather sparse human bones as representing the spoils of battle, the victorious inhabitants having decapitated the enemy and set the heads upon poles at the entrance to the settlement. By the time Boyd Dawkins came to write his report on the human remains for the Glastonbury Lake Village monograph, he had altered his view, and Bulleid disagreed with this as well, as we will see.

The British Association provided a large amount of support to the work, year by year, and it often received a lecture on the Lake Village at its Annual Meeting. Munro or Boyd Dawkins generally performed this function, but not to universal approval. Occasionally it seemed to some that the mantle of work *done* as well as that of popular dissemination was being assumed too frequently, and Bulleid was warned. In 1896 the Association was to meet in Toronto (of all places) and he received a letter from a friend:

> 'Do you intend to go to Toronto next year with the British Association? If so I recommend you to take your slides and exhibit them yourself – if you do not go – lend them to me, and give me any new information; it shall then be made clear *who* has done the work – my friend Dr Munro made a hash at Liverpool and even that was interesting – he ought to confine himself to what *he knows*.'

This was the same Munro who had earnestly entreated Bulleid to stick to the facts at all times.

In 1897 Bulleid narrowly escaped being buried alive when a wall of peat and clay fell onto him as he was drawing a section. In the same year he received a letter that may not have seemed so momentous as the escape, but which nonetheless was profoundly significant to Bulleid's life.

> 'October 29 1897 Blandford
>
> My dear sir,
> Weather permitting I am thinking of cycling over to Glastonbury at the weekend, hoping to see something of the results of your researches in the Lake Dwellings at Godney. You will perhaps remember my visit to Glastonbury one Sunday in April 1895, when you were so kind as to devote an hour or so to me in the Museum. You will identify me as General Pitt Rivers' assistant. As regards archaeology I hope that I am now beginning to creep into knowledge now that I have been with the General for 9 years ...
>
> Yours very truly
> Harold St Geo Gray'.

Gray was to become Bulleid's colleague, and co-director, for almost 40 years, of Lake Village research in Somerset.

## Postponement 1898 -1904

By the end of the excavations of 1897, Bulleid had reached a position both emotionally and physically that suggested the time was near when he should re-assess his plans for the site as well as for his own self. He wrote to Munro:

> 'I think it will be the better plan to stop work altogether at the end of the coming summer at least for a season or two - to give me an opportunity of preparing things for publishing - but I intend ultimately to finish the whole settlement.'

There was an enormous burden of finds accumulating in his father's house and the Museum. There was a third of the Lake Village still to excavate, with resulting finds requiring storage and preservation as well as study and illustration. The Museum at Glastonbury was in a state of neglect with far fewer visitors than the hundreds who had thronged in the early years. His father J G L Bulleid was no longer the major force in the Society or Town and, perhaps, was already beginning to be engulfed in misfortune both financial and physical. The collections, however, were probably the main cause of concern, and discussions were being held with the British Museum over an allocation of some specimens to London. The Committee of Reference and Advice was divided on this, Munro and Boyd Dawkins averse to any distribution, the two Arthurs (Evans and Bulleid) raising no objection to the dissemination of some artefacts duplicated in the collections. Bulleid wrote 'my only desire is that the objects should be safely housed and exhibited'. At Glastonbury they were not, and by 1899 Bulleid and so formidable a figure as John Morland were in favour of transferring the whole lot, not just duplicates, to Taunton. In the event this did not happen. Bulleid wrote:

> 'You may perhaps wonder at my wishing to see the collection housed elsewhere than at Glastonbury. I would not wish it if I knew in years to come the things would be cared for and appreciated. There is not a person in the neighbourhood who is capable of handling the specimens besides Mr Morland and Tom Paul the labourer I should say friend who has worked with me all the time.'

13. *Annie Bulleid*

## Annie Austin and Dymboro (AG)

In the mid 1890s Bulleid had become acquainted with the Austin family from Australia who had come to Glastonbury for an extended visit. The Abbey House in Glastonbury was inhabited by James and Rebecca Austin. James had had an adventurous life in Australia, made his fortune (along with other Austins he held over 200,000 acres in various sheep stations) and returned to England to retire to his native Somerset. At the time, Albert Austin and his wife Catherine with two daughters Annie and Kitty came from Australia to Glastonbury to visit their cousins. Albert and James were first cousins. The Bulleids and the Abbey House Austins

14. *Dymboro under construction*

were good friends. Arthur Bulleid's discovery and the excavations were the talk of the town and the Albert Austins were soon acquainted with the Bulleids and my father's work in the field. My mother and father became friends. My father had a very sweet tenor voice and he visited the Abbey House frequently; my mother played the piano, my father sang. Friendship developed into love and they became engaged. Grandfather Austin did not approve of his daughter marrying a penniless archaeologist and he took her back to Australia. My father returned to his medical studies and after several years he sent a cable 'Qualified'. My mother crossed the seas once again and they were married on 27th September 1900 at All Souls, Langham Place, London. After qualifying my father took several locums.

Dr Alexander Waugh was a Physician of Midsomer Norton in north Somerset. Dr Waugh retired and my father acquired his practice. My mother and father started their married life in a small house in North Road, Midsomer Norton, then they moved to The Old Vicarage which was larger and central, opposite the Church and Post Office. All the while a permanent home was being built, Grandfather Austin's wedding present to my mother and father. *Dymboro* was designed by Rupert Austin an architect and a cousin of my mothers, the builders were Longs of Bath; Mr Stamp was the foreman and local men were used for the work. My mother disagreed with some of the layout of the house proposed by the architect; she wanted the stairs to be out of sight of the front door. The architect said this was impossible, given the shape of the building. My mother said 'I will make it possible' and did so. It was a very beautiful house and home.

Midsomer Norton was then a dull unattractive place, a mining community. The miners were underpaid and badly housed, and there was much poverty. The local community accepted my parents and family and I personally was told that 'the big house was a greatly appreciated and admired addition to the village and my parents much loved'. One example of the last was only revealed in 1951.

> 'Dear Sirs
> About 40 years ago you attended my wife at the confinement of her second child. We were in very poor circumstances as I never had a regular wage, being dependant on the weather. You never sent us the bill for same and we both put it down that you knew our poor financial position. I believe your fee at that time was £1. I am enclosing £2 to settle this account and may God Almighty bless you the remainder of your days.
>
> Yours very respectfully
> an OAP '

A close friend of Armynell Bulleid was Mary Flower, who has described Dymboro.

> 'Coming from my London home, I was thrilled by this spacious house. The floors and doors were of golden, polished hardwood. The wide corridor, in which the children had played hockey, was brightened by several woven rugs brought back from Yugoslavia, the embrasures of the windows contained handsome oriental ginger jars and baskets full of flowers. The whitewashed walls, which had never been papered, were hung with Mrs. Bulleid's beautiful flower paintings, mostly in watercolour; large, fresh and vivid. One could smell the wallflowers, primroses and velvety roses, and feel the sharp, vigorous thorns. Indeed, the scent of flowers

filled the whole house, coming in through the big windows from the beautiful great garden, burgeoning with blossom and bees, and offset by the wide view across the valley. How lovely it all was.'

15. *A clay floor of mound 74 under excavation in 1906*

Arthur and Annie Bulleid settled into their life at Dymboro, the doctor combining his medical practice with his archaeological interests, and Mrs Bulleid managing the house and raising a large family.

'We were an odd family, six of us divided into two groups of three with a five-year-gap. The three eldest were born 1902-4-6 and the next three 1910-12-15. In fact it was sometimes thought that my mother had been married twice. I believe the three eldest knew our father better than the second trio. Life was easier then, no shortage of money from Australia, there were family connections to visit in and near Glastonbury and there were outings with our father, long nature walks, catching butterflies. Nevertheless my father did have long periods of depression; he worried about money and thought my mother's life style too pretentious. My father must have had his father's bankruptcy on his mind at times.'(AG)

## Harold St. George Gray and new excavations 1904-07

The Glastonbury Lake Village remained untouched from 1898 to 1904 other than by a small excavation carried out in 1902, not by Bulleid but by Harold St. George Gray. Gray, formerly assistant to Lt. General Pitt Rivers and with long experience in excavations, had just been appointed Assistant Secretary of the Somerset Archaeological and Natural History Society as well as Curator of the Society's Museum. At the request of the Society, and with the permission of the owner of the site (the Glastonbury Antiquarian Society), he opened up trenches across two of the mounds, cutting into the central hearth areas.

By 1903 Bulleid was ready to resume excavations in the Lake Village, and work commenced in May 1904. The excavations were now jointly directed by Bulleid and Gray. In theory this was a good team, and in practice it seems to have worked. Bulleid was particularly interested in structures, and in the environmental and economic base of the

16. *The hearth on floor 1 of mound 67 at Glastonbury in 1906*

settlement. Gray was interested in the small finds, of pottery and bone and stone, but especially those of metal and glass. Because both men had full-time jobs, as doctor and curator respectively, they could only excavate for short periods of time each year, generally four weeks in late May and early June. Their annual reports which appear in the relative issues of the Somerset Archaeological and Natural History Society *Proceedings* are detailed and give more information about the particular mounds and finds than appear in the final monographs on the site. The aim of Bulleid and Gray was to work as steadily as possible and to complete the excavation of the entire site by 1907. Funds were in short supply by the end but a timely gesture on the part of one or two individuals allowed six weeks of work in 1907, and Bulleid then wrote 'The systematic examination of the entire village is now complete, with the exception of a small piece of ground on which the shed stands.' It was a quite extraordinary achievement on the part of Bulleid in particular, but also of Tom Paul the leader of the labouring team and someone entrusted with more than mere trench digging. And it was not always easy. In 1904 the rain was excessive and on one day, June 3, excursions by three societies had to be abandoned due to the drenching rain; a week earlier another party had shared the same fate. There is little sign that the excavation team ever paused for such inconveniences as water from above; it was groundwater, floods, that sometimes forced abandonment. The cost of the entire excavation, 1893-1907, was £697-19-0, Bulleid having taken no salary whatsoever throughout the time. A grateful Glastonbury Antiquarian Society elected him President 1908-1924.

## Publication of the Glastonbury Lake Village report

Bulleid and Gray were now, 1907, faced with a daunting task - to publish the results of eleven years of excavation on a site full of structural remains, deep deposits, and extremely rich in finds; pencil plans and sections existed in Bulleid's notebooks, and he had already reconstructed a large-scale plan of the site upon which he was able to put the find-spots of small artefacts. Gray had his own set of notebooks and a 'black book' in which he entered lists of finds, arranged by categories such as Objects of Bone, of Baked-Clay, of Glass, Spindle-Whorls and Weaving Combs. Pottery had already been separated into Decorated and Plain vessels, with the latter receiving relatively little attention; this was in opposition to the strictures of Pitt Rivers but the quantities were very great. Bulleid counted about 4400

*17. Publication drawings of 'Glastonbury ware' by Bulleid*

unornamented vessels (represented by many thousands of pot sherds) and about 800 decorated pots. Yet by neglecting to assign each potsherd a number and a 'layer' in its mound, the possibility of using sherds to relate the layers from adjoining mounds was lost. Bulleid was particularly interested in pottery; he had had some training, was an excellent draughtsman, and actually made many pots himself, most alas now lost. His research into decorated Iron Age pottery led him to visit over thirty museums in Britain where he made drawings and notes on relevant material.

Through the years of work at Glastonbury there was a constant exchange of letters with specialists who might report on particular subjects, with those concerned with the organisation of the monograph, and with those able to help with finance for the publication. Gray was as determined as Bulleid to get the final report under way, although in 1905 he had written 'what with Glastonbury, Cornwall and Weston, my arrears here are simply appalling; but I am making no attempt to clear up everything at once; indeed it would be an impossibility.' His arrears never did deter him from excavating until he was well over 80 years of age, and his 'legacy' remains with us today.

In 1908 Bulleid and Gray started to organize the final report and Munro was asked to contribute the Introductory Chapter, a title it retained. Munro was prompt in submitting the text and then pressed for speedy publication. As early as summer 1908 he wrote 'you ought to have appointed an Editor to bring the contributions to the scratch otherwise I am afraid the Monograph will be long in coming.' Both Bulleid and Gray were responsible for the monograph,

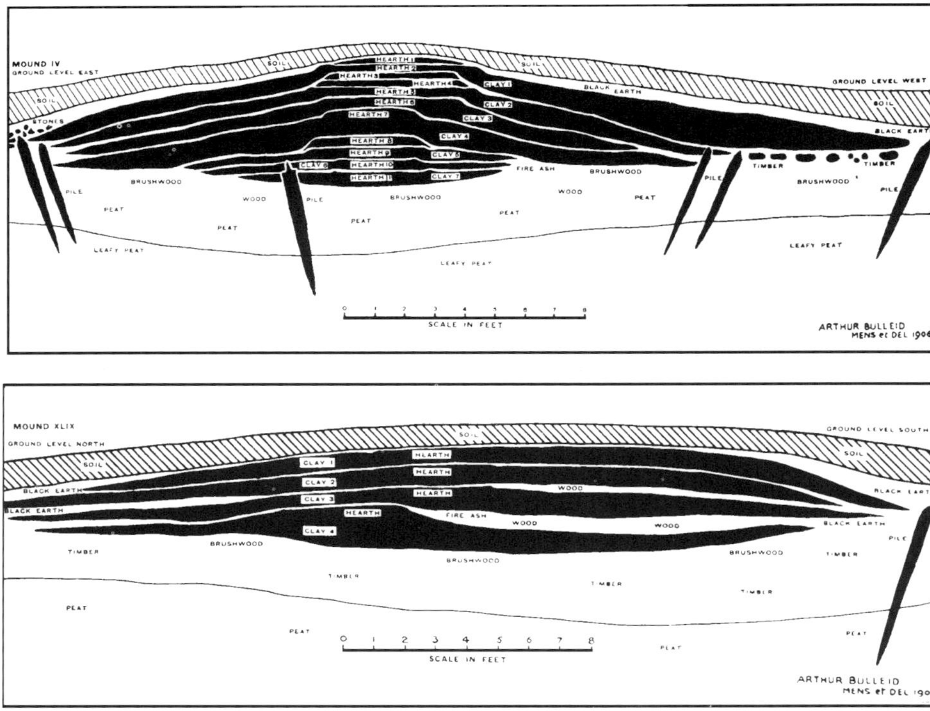


18. *Sections through mounds 4 and 49 showing the superimposed floors and hearths*

of course, but by early 1910 Gray appears to have assumed that he was doing most of the editorial work. He wrote to Munro setting out exactly who was doing what and concluded '*Nominally* both Bulleid and myself are Editors, but *really* all Editorial work will be under my charge. I shall be responsible for seeing the great book through the Press ...' In early 1911 Bulleid and Gray announced the price for the two volumes of royal quarto : £2-2-0 for orders prior to the appearance of volume one, £2-12-6 thereafter up to the appearance of volume two, when the price became an incredible £3-3-0. After a slight delay, *The Glastonbury Lake Village* volume 1 appeared in 1911, to universal acclaim. This was and remains the more important of the pair; volume two appeared in 1917. Gray was put in charge of sending out copies to the subscribers who numbered almost 300, from The Hon. John Abercromby to Worcester Massachusetts (The Clark University). Copies were sent to all parts of the world: 'The Australian volumes are packed and addressed for the next sailing of P and O'. (HSGG)

The book contained a grateful acknowledgement to Tom

19. *Bulleid made a detailed plan of the Glastonbury Lake Village excavations plotting the positions of structures and artefacts*

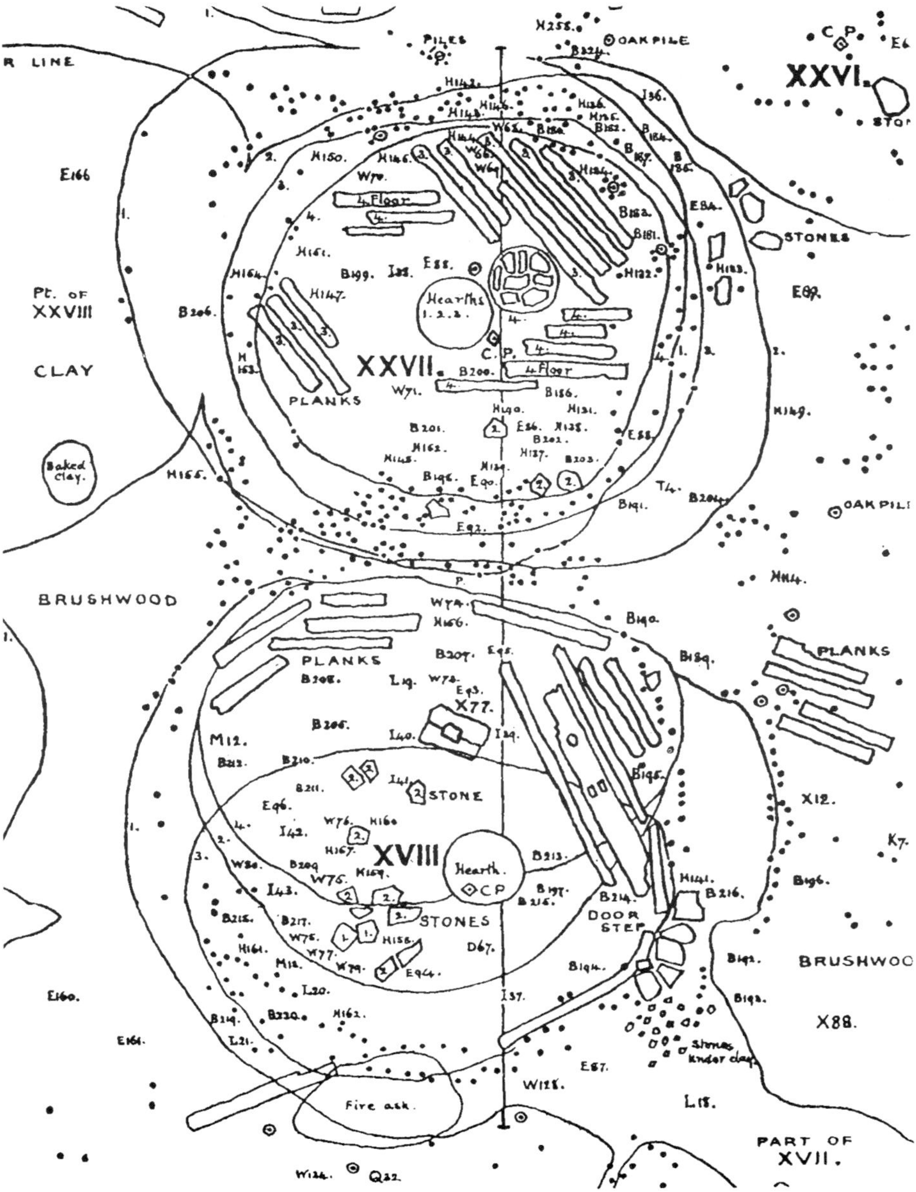
PILES
OAK PILE
C.P.
XXVI.
E166
Pt. of
XXVIII
CLAY
Baked clay.
4 Floor
Hearths 1.2.3.
XXVII
C.P.
4 Floor
PLANKS
STONES
OAK PILE
BRUSHWOOD
PLANKS
X77.
STONE
XVIII
Hearth.
CP
STONES
DOOR STEP
PLANKS
X12.
Stones under clay
Fire ash.
X88.
PART OF
XVII.

Paul 'whose interest in the excavation never failed from beginning to end. He removed the first turf, and was the last to leave the field upon completion of the exploration.' There were twenty-nine chapters in the two volumes, 101 plates, 179 drawings and 724 pages - all for £2-2-0. The volumes are now rarely seen for sale, and fetch large sums of money when they do come up. Bulleid contributed the major chapter on a Description of the Lake Village, mound by mound, illustrated by his own plans and sections. He also wrote about the environment, the wooden objects, the pottery, querns and stones. Lawrence Bulleid, his brother, contributed a colour frontispiece of a selection of the glass beads. Gray contributed 14 chapters on all the other finds, and various specialists (most of them Fellows of the Royal Society or other high order) supplied chapters on animals and plants. The final two chapters were by Boyd Dawkins on the inhabitants of the village, their racial and linguistic characters, and here he proposed the idea that the village had been terminated not by natural events such as flooding but by a massacre of the occupants. It took Bulleid a number of years to dispose of this theory which had no basis in any of the evidence that Bulleid had recovered so carefully. As editor, Bulleid must have been sorely tempted to amend Boyd Dawkins' fanciful theory, but he was too polite to tamper with the text of the Professor.

## The Glastonbury Lake Village

Our current view of the Glastonbury Lake Village, based upon Bulleid and Gray's total excavation, and fortified by more recent research, is that the village was constructed in the last two centuries B.C. by a group of settlers arriving from we-know-not-where, but probably from the hills and uplands that edge the low-lying moors and swamps. Upon a patch of fenwood about two thirds of a mile from the dryland of Glastonbury itself, where stands the Tor and Abbey ruins, the settlers dumped huge quantities of logs, brushwood, stones and clay, most of it brought to the site by boat or raft, or dragged across somewhat less soggy patches of swampland. Around this base was set a palisade, a substantial fence of upright logs entirely surrounding the village except for one break towards the west; the logs were up to 14 feet long and were driven into the underlying peat and clay. Bulleid spent some time investigating how such piles could have been driven so firmly into place. He wrote a brief account of 'the human pile driver' method as observed in North Borneo: Sharpen the pole; fasten two poles horizontally to the pole at right angles to one another at a height from pole base equal to the depth to be driven plus depth of any water; position four men to steady the pole; position eight men on the horizontals (two on each arm); 'their weight with a gentle swaying does the rest - unless they meet a rock!'

There was a causeway running out on the east, probably a landing stage for boats using the sluggish waters of the Brue River or one of its meandering tributaries. Inside the palisade was the village, a collection of buildings set upon clay spreads and floors, with perhaps 4 or 5 separate sets of buildings, and pathways and open spaces between. The main domestic houses were circular in plan, each with a thick clay floor, hearth, wattle and daub walls and thatched roof. Some had wooden floors, and parts of timber doors with pivot points suggest that other wooden components such as low platform beds, benches and tables may have existed - there were heaps of broken and discarded woodwork littering some of the houses and dumps. The floors were often renewed, and hearths too, so that layer upon layer of floors were built up over time, as the weight of the house caused gradual subsidence into the wet substructure and underlying peat. The entrance to some houses was paved with stones or wood, and one or two houses had porches. The hearths were sometimes quite elaborate - they must have been focal points for many activities, cooking, eating, working at various crafts during the poor weather or dark, sleeping, visiting and talking. Some houses had ovens, sunk into the floor, and when found were filled with ash and charcoal. The round houses were from 18 to 28 feet in diameter, giving a good area inside. Bulleid always believed that not all of the 90 'mounds' at Glastonbury had been round dwelling houses, and could point to various clay 'floors' with no trace of posts or walling. He also thought that there had been square buildings as well as round houses with clay floors. In this he was eagerly, indeed constantly and persuasively, supported by John Morland who wrote a stream of letters starting in 1906. Morland believed there were two phases of settlement at the Lake Village, an earlier with morticed beam structures, oak piles and hurdlework, and a later with round wattle huts and almost all of the domestic debris; 'the passage from rectangular huts to round huts seems to me to be a change of the first order,

20. *The modern view of Glastonbury Lake Village is that only a proportion of the buildings were in use at any one time*

not a change of fashion, but of people'. In the monograph, Bulleid did not pursue this question very fully, but he did add a footnote stating that the rectangular huts were not of the same age as the round huts, but were put on the site first, yet he made the point that nowhere was a complete rectangular hut found *in situ*, but only fragments of timbers and hurdles.

This is not the place for an essay on re-interpretation of the Lake Village structures or organisation. There have been several attempts made, one concentrating on the existence

21. *Model made by Bulleid of a Glastonbury Lake Village house*

of an earlier settlement with square or rectangular houses, and one concerned with the social organization of the settlement. We do not think that either of these theses stands up to serious examination of the details in each, and indeed are quite fundamentally flawed, but each has advanced new concepts that are valuable:

1. that the rectangular huts may mark specific activities separate from those of the round houses
2. that the settlement was organized into separate household units and delimited areas.

Bulleid foreshadowed both of these ideas in his own sparsely-worded interpretive notes; his square houses are noted above, and he wrote, 'it has been conjectured, the occupation began with four or five dwellings, and that the entire Village was a gradual extension and growth around them'.

The debris recovered from the Lake Village is truly outstanding in the light of Iron Age material culture. Few if any sites in Britain have yielded such a variety and abundance of finds and any modern study of artefacts begins with the Glastonbury evidence. The reason why so much material was found, and in such good condition, is due to the wetness of the site and its softness. Swampy ground, peat and watery reed beds all provided a comfortable home for any objects deliberately dumped outside the palisade, and objects accidentally dropped within the settlement often came to rest within soft and damp clay, or the organic mud that squeezed up around the clay spreads. Domestic equipment included well-made pottery as well as coarser wares, wooden tools and vessels, woven baskets, iron implements, stone grinders and pounders, weaving-combs and spindle whorls; more personal objects, owned and perhaps attached to individuals, included glass beads, shale armlets, bronze brooches and other trinkets. Perhaps for communal use were ladders, anvils, dugout canoes, and horse harness. Wheels and axles for carts or waggons were made, but the vehicles were probably in use elsewhere, on the mainland. Domestic animals, cattle, sheep and pigs, were kept and hunting wild animals was an important activity. Fields for grazing and cultivation were on the dryland islands of Godney or the mainland to the south. All of the evidence points to a well-organised prosperous village, probably beginning as a small

*22. Bulleid washing pottery in the Glastonbury excavations site hut*

hamlet with only a few families, then rapidly growing as the crannog base was extended and the palisade was enlarged to encompass the whole village of, perhaps, 20 families. The end came, not by a massacre but by a gradual waterlogging of the whole area; the villagers could contend with flooding in winter, but when the floods became severe and never-ending, it was time to go, back to the uplands.

Before leaving the Glastonbury Lake Village it is worth noting that Bulleid's observations, as he recorded them, have almost always been found to be accurate. Sir Harry Godwin commented more than once on Bulleid's acute knowledge of the environment of the village, obtained through his own borings on a line from the dryland of Glastonbury to Godney island. And his description of the round houses and the sequence of deposits, mound by mound, are informative and can serve as the basis for modern constructions of 'Glastonbury huts'. Of course, methods of excavation and analysis have advanced since 1892 but without exception modern scholars have come to rely upon the records of these excavations that were far in advance of their time – who of Bulleid' s contemporaries in 1900 concentrated upon environment and economy, on open-plan excavation, on scientific analyses, and on a measured factual account of a total site excavation, and published the lot?

## Excavations at Meare Village West 1909-32

Note has already been made of the discovery of the lake village at Meare in 1895. In fact, when Bulleid first visited Farmer Laver's fields he noticed two mounded areas, which he called Meare Village West and Meare Village East. In 1908, following the conclusion of the work at Glastonbury, Bulleid took two men and went to Meare to put in an exploratory trench across one of the mounds. 'This small digging yielded more objects than were found in many of the larger Glastonbury dwellings. There were few spadefuls of earth that did not contain something of archaeological value. Fragments of pottery and bones of animals alone filled several wheelbarrows.' As a result of this, Munro hurried down from Scotland and wrote an account for *The Times* - history repeated. The Somerset Archaeological and Natural History Society set up a Meare Committee to organize excavations and the British Association established a Lake Village sub-Committee to do likewise. Thus encour-

*23. Tom Paul standing in front of a section through mound 7 at Meare Village West*

aged and supported, Bulleid and Gray embarked on a long series of excavations at Meare Village West, 1909-1932, the war years excluded. The mounded settlement was excavated with the rap method, long trenches cut and adjoining trenches then cut so that the soil from the second trench could be thrown into the first, and so on, as work progressed; this saved time and money at the end of each season, when the fields were returned to a uniform state.

Teams of 6 to 8 men were employed, with Tom Paul again leading the men. In the beginning he was paid 5/0, the labourers 3/6 and a boy 1/3, for a day of work that began at 7.30 am and ended at 6 pm. By 1926 inflation had set in and the daily earnings were 9/4 for the foreman (alas, no longer Tom Paul) and 6/8 for the labourers. In 1914 Bulleid again lectured to the Society of Antiquaries where he presented the latest results from Meare; in 1917 the second volume of the Glastonbury report appeared and he, and Gray, were congratulated by many, e.g. 'it is a perfect joy', 'it is refreshing to get a candid, careful and conscientious scientific treatment.' By 1920, however, problems at Meare emerged, mostly of the financial kind. Although support continued to come from a number of sources, Gray in

24. *Timber substructure of mounds 12, 13 and 14 at Meare Village West in 1912*

particular was chafing at the limited amount of funds; he wrote Bulleid in 1921 'What is the use of these new brooms on the Lake Village B.A. Committee, unless they vote us some money to do the work. Beyond printing a short report... and making a grant - sometimes - the B.A. Committee is absolutely useless to us except to bring forward young antiquarians ...' We don't know who these young antiquarians are, or were. The reorganised Committee did not include one of the major figures in British field archaeology, O.G.S. Crawford, who declined to join and wrote Bulleid saying that he felt that excavating another Lake Village in Somerset would not add new information, and

25. *Bulleid addressing the Somerset Archaeological and Natural History Society on the occasion of their visit to Meare West in 1926*

the money should go elsewhere, to new projects in Holderness, Yorkshire. He did, however, send Bulleid practical information on how to contour a mound.

The team of Bulleid and Gray continued to operate at Meare Village West for 4 to 6 weeks each year, Gray being released from his duties at Taunton for the purpose. A letter from Bulleid to the Society explained how important this release was: 'not only on account of his experience but because of his special care to the finds (their cataloguing and restoration)... During the excavations there is a constant round of duties which are far more than one director can carry out effectively.' And Bulleid also had his medical practice, and growing family, to help fill his days.

## Life at Dymboro (AG)

Life at Dymboro revolved round my father - his doctoring and excavating on the Somerset Levels. His was a busy life. We did not have family holidays but went down to Meare when the excavation was in progress. We stayed with the Misses Burnett one fat, one thin. We were not allowed to drink local water, to our delight we drank quantities of ginger beer a great treat. We went to the excavation nearly every day and found it rather boring. My mother sketched and talked to visitors. We were not at all interested or impressed by the well known people who visited the field and we soon tired of washing pottery.

When my father felt relaxed and had the time he was amusing and original - he could stand on his head and one evening when we were play acting and dressing up he appeared as 'Mr Back to Front' how he contrived the transformation I do not know, I was very young, someone must have helped him dress up but I remember a mask drawn on paper and of course coat, waistcoat, collar and tie back to front. I believe my father and his peers in Glastonbury did enjoy themselves - they acted and had picnics and sang in Gilbert and Sullivan productions. My father had a very sweet voice and I remember lying in bed as a child and listening to him singing in the drawing room below. Our governess played the piano. He sang old ballads. He was athletic and played a good game of tennis. I remember him playing on the court at Dymboro but unfortunately he strained a ligament in his leg and that was the end of playing tennis - he was small and spritely and got around the court at great speed. There were happy Sunday evenings in winter round the study fire roasting chestnuts and playing pencil and paper games -'Heads, bodies and legs' was a favourite and also 'Consequences'. We were often joined by Evelyn Waugh, grandson of Dr. Alexander Waugh. Evelyn came to stay with his three maiden Aunts in Midsomer Norton. He was the same age as my elder brother Hilary, he was witty, he and the family could draw and there was much merriment. Evelyn was not pleasant; he teased me and actively disliked my younger brother Humfrey but my sister Bettrys (Betty) was his girl friend.

My mother and father must have had their 'ups and downs' but we were not aware of quarrels and they did not lose their tempers 'in front of the children'. We had lunch at 1.00 pm. My father would come in from his 'round' if all was well he would go quickly into his cloakroom and then join us in the dining room. If he was upset and had had a bad morning the front door would slam and he would go straight into the surgery and that door would slam. Perhaps he would go to the study to use the telephone and would not come into lunch at all. On these occasions we children would keep quiet. On one occasion a servant spoke of the 'piercing eye of the doctor' and this piercing eye kept the six of us in order most of the time and I never knew

*26. Annie and Arthur Bulleid (right) on the Somerset Archaeological and Natural History Society's visit to Ammerdown House, near Radstock, in 1911*

my father to chastise any member of the family.

As well as 'the study' my father had a bedroom upstairs which was known as 'the pottery room'. There he would work away reconstructing pots from the excavations. There were bags and bags of pottery all carefully numbered with the mound they came from, tins of plaster of Paris, and a glue pot. No one ever tidied 'the pottery room'. There was a climbing rose outside the window in which fly catchers nested every year, the tennis net a favourite perch.

He did most of his writing at night sitting up till 2.00 and 3.00 am. He had a peat fire and smoked his pipe - Smiths Glasgow Mixture. He said he could hear spiders walking! The polished oak floors were not carpeted and I expect the boards creaked! In old age he suffered from cold and cold feet and said to me he wished he was in a little almshouse where he could keep warm.

My father had a delightful sense of humour and from time to time he would have a funny story to tell. He would start off and then burst out laughing before he had reached the point, he would calm down and continue to the end but later on he would burst out laughing again; we the family would laugh at him laughing more than laughing at his joke. He dreamt one night he was playing football, he was kicking goals, and kicking my mother. Mother was not amused;

it was not done to talk about people in bed together!

One day he was driving his bull-nosed Morris and he hit a man on a bicycle - the man fortunately was not hurt and landed sitting astride the bonnet of the car - my father found this very amusing, my mother was shocked!

My father was always nervous when he lectured or spoke in public. I went with him when he gave the Long Fox Memorial Lecture - he took my hand when walking from the car park to the lecture hall clutching at me spasmodically his hands damp with sweat. He started his lecture very hesitantly but as he warmed to his subject and his audience the words flowed easily and he was loath to stop - eventually the Chairman had to bring the meeting to a close.

I was at home for weekends from school and I often went with my father over Mendip to the Somerset Levels. He introduced me to coffee with lots of sugar. One outing I remember particularly we went to the Burtle Beds. We were armed with cocoa tins on long strings and we sat on the edge of the quarry dangled our tins over the edge and pulled them up scraping against the quarry face. It was in that manner that a rare shell was discovered much to the delight of Dr Wilfred Jackson. Although I was shy with my father other people were not and he was constantly consulted on all kinds of topics and folk would call with objects and items for his opinion.

My parents were public spirited. They started a local Nursing Association. My mother sat on the Board of Guardians. My father ran a Chess Club once a fortnight - twelve tables - we children would arrange the tables and chairs in the drawing room and would serve tea and coffee and buns half way through the evening - I remember the thick atmosphere of pipe and cigarette smoke, the fishy smell of the fish monger and the raw meaty smell of the butcher and how thankful we were to open the windows when everyone had gone.

At some stage wasps became a real pest and my father let it be known that he would pay a certain amount for every queen wasp brought to him. I don't know how much - a penny perhaps three pence? This had wonderful results and the wasp nuisance was much reduced. The tradespeople were very grateful. My mother had a Fete in the garden annually for the Nursing Association and she had a stall at the Church Bazaar for missions.

My father was known and respected for his diagnoses. He once diagnosed a case of smallpox and with quick action

*27. Dr Bulleid with staff of Paulton Hospital*

on his part I believe there was only one isolated case. Consultants came from Bristol to advise my father if he was worried about a particular patient. On one occasion a gentleman stayed for an evening meal, my mother consistently called him Mr X. Afterwards my father said to her 'My dear Annie you know our guest was Mr Y and Mr X and Mr Y do not like each other at all!' This was one of my father's funny stories at my mother's expense.

My father was very germ conscious - we as children had to wear gloves when travelling and we were seldom allowed to go to the local Fair for fear of infection. He rebuked my mother when she took out her handkerchief and dusted an ornament or a bit of furniture as she passed!

My father had strong dislikes: blood sports, ladies wearing earrings, he said they were barbaric, cats, pit owners and crooners. He was very interested in 'the wireless' and he would 'listen in' for long periods twiddling the cat's whisker-it was then that he heard crooners and popular dance bands he would grumble but he still went on listening. Although against blood sports he had a shot gun and would shoot bullfinches because they ate the buds from the fruit trees. He once opened up a little bird to show us the crop full of gooseberry buds.

My mother was a delightful hostess and a clever raconteur, and guests enjoyed visiting Dymboro. My father would be fairly quiet during meal times but once the meal was over he and his archaeological friend or friends would disappear into the study – the door firmly shut and talk would begin.

A constant visitor was Father Ethelbert Horne, titular Abbot of Glastonbury, who lived at Downside Abbey, Stratton-on-the-Fosse. He was particularly fond of grapefruit and when he came the meal always began with grapefruit. My mother once addressed him as Father Grapefruit. The family found it very difficult to keep straight faces but I believe ever afterwards Father Horne was known as Father Grapefruit. Another visitor much loved was Dr Wilfred Jackson – my mother loved his north country accent.

Later in life when I was married to Geoffrey Goodall, Canon of Salisbury Cathedral, my father and he had discussions about the Lord's Prayer and the Creed; various points had worried my father from his school days. My father could not accept the service of the Holy Communion the idea of taking the Body and Blood of Christ was unacceptable. At home underdone meat was refused and should a joint show blood out it would go back to the kitchen. Only once do I remember my father going to Church he came to Mattins with us when we were on a family holiday at Looe after the 1914-18 war and this is in fact the only family holiday I remember.

My father loved the garden but he did not have enough time to do much gardening. He pruned fruit trees and picked apples and pears. He grew Lilium Regali from seed with great success. He kept the Yew hedges trimmed during the 1914-18 war which was a hard and trying task - the lawns went to hay. My father set up a little distillery in the surgery each year and distilled lavender water, this was an annual event and much appreciated by my mother. He was very fond of asparagus and it was considered a treat - the grown ups would have it for their evening meal my father would bring me up a few spears with melted butter and I would sit up in bed and eat it, a very special treat!

All my life my father was teetotal but had not always been so. A patient was an alcoholic and killing himself - this gentleman said to my father 'If you will give up drinking I will'. They shook hands. The patient lived a long and happy life, I remember him. My mother and father, my sister Christine and I went to Australia for six months, we were in Marseille for my 21st birthday - we had a lovely meal on shore and my father ordered a bottle of wine and he drank my health - the one and only time I saw him take a drink.

## Fieldwork and research 1921 - 38

The excavations at the Meare sites and the subsequent finds processing and writing up must have occupied much of Bulleid's time outside his medical duties. Yet, remarkably, he was involved in a wide variety of other archaeological activities. These ranged from a brief visit and the collection of a few sherds of pottery or flints found lying on the surface, to assisting others in their excavations and to excavations of his own, some on a large scale.

In 1921 Bulleid began a prolific archaeological association and close friendship with Ethelbert Horne of Downside Abbey. Keynsham parish churchyard reached its limit for burials in 1877. Two and a half acres of meadowland to the north of Keynsham, adjacent to what is now the A4175, was purchased to serve as a new cemetery. Unknowingly this land concealed the site of a Roman villa. Grave diggers frequently encountered difficulties in carrying out their work. The lower courses of walls and floors had to be 'bumped through'. In June 1921 upon hearing of this Bulleid and Horne paid a visit to the cemetery when they witnessed the sexton destroy part of a flight of steps. Having seen this and gained some idea of the extent of the building Bulleid and Horne determined to excavate before all that lay within the cemetery was destroyed. The Keynsham Excavation Committee was formed with Bulleid and Horne the joint directors. Careful and delicate discussions took place. In spite of the close proximity of recent graves the parish council gave their approval to the project. Excavations took place over a period of ten weeks over three seasons from 1922 to 1924. During that time one or other of the directors was always on site, Bulleid taking specific responsibility for drawing. Fry and Sons, chocolate manufacturers in Keynsham, helped finance the work and loaned equipment. Seven men were employed.

What emerged was a particularly large and wealthy courtyard villa on a par with the better known Woodchester and Chedworth villas. Work concentrated on the north and west wings and revealed that the building was at least 270 by 230 feet. Regrettably their strategy was to follow walls and mosaics with no attention paid to areas outside the main buildings and to view the villa as single phase with no attempt to investigate its development over time. The positions of finds, important dating evidence, were not recorded and little pottery was saved. The discovery of sixteen mosaics gives an idea of the villa's wealth. Some had been totally destroyed, represented by quantities of displaced tesserae, others survived remarkably intact. Particularly fine

28. *A mosaic floor in the west corridor of Keynsham villa. Bulleid is seated drawing on the middle left edge of the picture*

was the mosaic in the 'hexagon room' with its geometric designs, birds, leaf sprays, fruit and figures which included Jupiter in the guise of a bull and Europa. At a meeting of the Keynsham Excavation Committee on 3rd August 1923 Bulleid recommended that the hexagon room be preserved *in situ* with a building placed over it and that the adjoining rooms be covered up and an outline in stone or cement be laid on the surface to mark the position of the walls. Unfortunately this line of action proved impossible. To ensure their survival, part of the hexagon room mosaic floor and the better preserved parts of others were lifted in 1924. Paid for by Frys, these panels remain in the factory which is now owned by Cadbury Schweppes. The results of the excavations were published by Bulleid and Horne in *Archaeologia* for 1924-25 which reveals that Bulleid also supported the work financially with a contribution of four guineas. While preparations were in progress for the above in 1922 a second Roman building was found during construction of a new Frys factory a short distance to the east. This too was excavated. Recent discoveries (1991) have shown this building to be part of a previously unknown settlement.

Shortly afterwards the Bulleid-Horne partnership became involved with excavating cemeteries. Initially this was on a small scale in 1925 following the discovery of 4 or 5 human skeletons in a small quarry on Barrow Hill, Buckland Dinham, near Frome. When he visited the site Horne requested that any further burials be left *in situ* to allow careful examination. A few days later they were on site following discovery of another burial. Dating to the 6th or 7th century AD the skeleton was accompanied by grave goods comprising 2 silver earrings, 2 pear-shaped beads of amethystine quartz, 2 round glass beads and 2 shell beads.

There followed a second site on a much larger scale. In the summer of 1926 workmen engaged in a quarry at Camerton came across several human skeletons. Near to one of them was an iron spearhead and knife. Bulleid and Horne undertook trial excavations after which the Camerton Excavation Committee was formed. Bulleid and Horne were initially appointed joint directors. Excavations lasted annually for about three weeks between 1928 and 1932. In an area covering 130 by 100 feet, 109 graves and 115 skeletons were found. All were orientated approximately east-west and some were accompanied by grave goods notably two gold bracteates, silver wire earrings, glass beads, enamelled hanging bowl escutcheons and iron knives. The cemetery spanned the late Roman period to the seventh century. The published report suggests that Horne took the lead role as it appears in his name only, although Bulleid receives a glowing acknowledgement for his contribution.

In 1930 the pair also excavated a Bronze Age round barrow at Pool Farm, West Harptree, prior to it being levelled. Over two weeks in September and October they revealed a stone cist containing a cremation. Bulleid took responsibility for planning the site.

Although Arthur Bulleid left Glastonbury for Midsomer Norton in 1900 his involvement with the archaeology of the former area continued. Not only did he remain active in the Glastonbury Antiquarian Society and its museum but he also undertook a number of excavations in the locality. These included a section across the large linear earthwork called Ponters Ball to the east of Glastonbury in 1909. A small quantity of pottery was found but in Bulleid's view '... it is neither wise nor advisable to suggest a definite date regarding the construction of the work until a further excavation is undertaken'. Further excavations took place in 1969 but were again inconclusive. With John Morland in 1926 Bulleid dug a 60 yard long trench through the low hill known as The Mound just to the south west of Glastonbury. They established that the hill was a natural feature and that it had been occupied in the prehistoric, Roman and medieval periods. In 1971 prior to levelling The

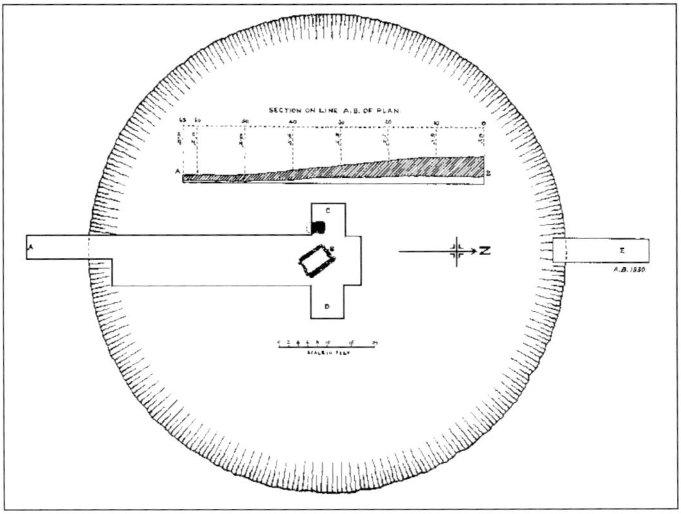


*29. Plan of Pool Farm barrow, West Harptree, excavated in 1930*

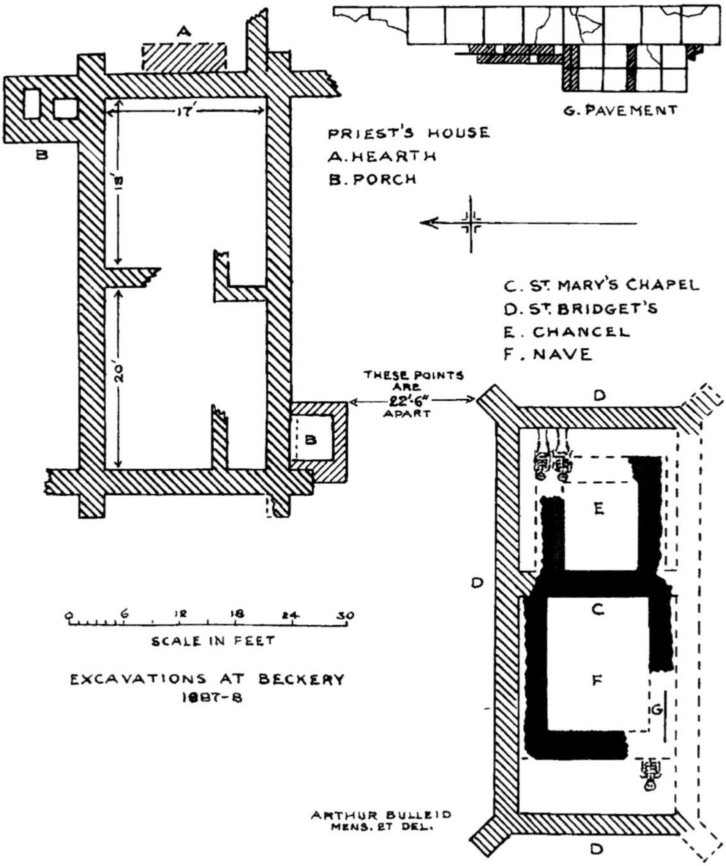


30. *Plan of the medieval chapel and priest's house excavated by John Morland at Beckery, Glastonbury, in 1887-8. Drawn by Bulleid, this plan is his earliest published archaeological work*

Mound there were more excavations. A Dark Age phase was identified but otherwise Bulleid's rather enigmatic evidence for occupation over a long period of time was confirmed.

Earthworks, particularly hillforts, were of interest to both Bulleid and Gray. The former was the leading figure in the formation of the Somerset Earthworks Committee. He canvassed a large number of people about the desirability of setting up a project to investigate earthworks within the county and the Committee was established in 1914. Twenty-two people were elected to the Committee including Professor Boyd Dawkins, Sir Hercules Read and Reginald Smith of the British Museum and the President of the Society of Antiquaries. Dawkins was elected president of the Committee, Bulleid secretary and Gray director of excavations. The First World War impeded progress and the committee never achieved as much as the founders had hoped for. In 1917 the main concern was Cannington Hillfort - it was threatened by quarrying for the mineral barytes, which was used in the manufacture of gun powder, but more immediately there was the problem of damage caused by the presence of 500 mules.

Excavations took place in 1918 at Dolebury Camp, Churchill, on the Neolithic long barrow at Murtry Hill, Buckland Dinham, in 1920 and Cadbury Camp, Tickenham in 1922. Bulleid was actively involved in the Murtry Hill work particularly surveying and photography. He made a contribution of £3-3-0 to the excavation funds. This was not the only occasion that Bulleid supported excavations financially; in 1907 he gave 5/- to work at Wick Barrow, Stogursey, in 1909 5/- to Charterhouse-on-Mendip, in 1913 5/- to South Cadbury hillfort, in 1926 £1 to Ham Hill and 1932 £5 to Meare Village West. In 1925 he donated £3-3-0 to excavations at Chelms Combe, Cheddar, directed by H E Balch and the Rev Palmer and, along with Horne, served on the excavation committee.

In 1923 the Ham Hill Excavation Committee was formed to investigate this enormous Iron Age hillfort in south Somerset. Under the chairmanship of Richard Hensleigh Walter membership included Professor Boyd Dawkins, Sir Hercules Read, Reginald Smith and Arthur Bulleid with Gray once again director of excavations. Bulleid visited the site on a number of occasions, usually in the company of Ethelbert Horne. On 19th July 1923 he was present when the site was visited by HRH The Prince of Wales. A letter dated 30th July 1923 from Walter shows that due to an oversight he was not introduced to the Prince:

> 'I told Gray especially to tell you that we had engaged a room at the inn for our friends for refreshment, rest and shelter, but he was so fully occupied in his ambition to 'bone' the Prince that apparently he neglected to tell people until too late. Mr Peacock, the Keeper of Records of the Duchy asked and expected me to present some of the Excavation Committee to the Prince, but Gray not having asked them to come to the inn as wished, this was not possible.'

Donations of finds to the Somerset County Museum and published notes reveal some of the many archaeological sites visited by Bulleid - Dundon Hill Camp, Kimmeridge, Dorset, Uphill and Kilmersdon Road Quarry, Radstock are but some. One of the earliest known examples was on 3rd March 1894 when, in company with his father and John Morland, he visited a quarry at Long Sutton which had produced archaeological material. When they arrived they were shown Romano-British pottery and a newly discovered skeleton lying *in situ* in a rock-cut grave; the quarrymen had already found two infant burials and two earthenware vessels containing cremations. On 28th November 1917 farmer Mr C Lippiatt discovered a stone coffin on land at Hill Farm, Priston. On the same day he wrote to Bulleid inviting him to visit. The offer was taken up and the coffin recorded and photographed. A report in *The Guardian* reveals that the burial received much attention 'During the weekend a big concourse of sightseers, numbering some hundreds, visited the field to see the coffin, among them miners and youths, and unfortunately some of them abused the opportunity causing considerable damage. Stones were flung into the coffin on top of the bones and a large piece was knocked out of one side of the coffin.' Just seven days after the Priston coffin was found, another one was discovered nearby at Midford which again required Bulleid's presence for recording.

In 1915 he donated three Roman brooches to the County Museum acquired from quarrymen at Haydon Quarry, Kilmersdon. Two had been found in 1913, the other had been discovered three years earlier since which time it had been worn in the finder's cap. He was always on the look out. In about 1911 he acquired a perforated macehead that had been found in 1842 south of Maesbury Camp on the parish border between Dinder and Croscombe. For forty years it had been one of many stones ornamenting a cottage windowsill. When, later, it was spotted by Bulleid in another house it was serving a different function - blocking a rat hole in the skirting board! Bulleid was convinced of the importance of recording as much information as possible. '... the writer firmly believes all archaeological finds, however unimportant they may appear at the time, should be permanently recorded in some way'.

Throughout the long years of work at Meare, Bulleid was active in establishing contacts with various specialists, just as he had done for the Glastonbury material. There were many seeds from Meare Village West and samples were sent off here and there for identification. An envelope

31. *Archaeological detail in Mark church, one of many sketches in the Bulleid notebooks*

survives, containing a few seeds, with the warning 'Grains of SPELT, don't sow this – I think it is too old to Germinate'. It presumably was – 2000 years.

In anticipation of human remains he felt obliged to write to Manchester Museum where Boyd Dawkins was based. A reply came from the museum, advising Bulleid that it would be better to let a young assistant work on the bones, as 'the old professor would have to learn over again to do the work on the latest lines.' In the event, very few human remains were found and no report was published. The absence of Iron Age cemeteries in the Levels always puzzled Bulleid and Gray. They occasionally sent out a couple of men to explore possible locations for the burials of the populations at the Glastonbury and Meare Lake Villages, but nothing was found. John Morland, still an active supporter of the work, suggested that at Meare, 'at any one time 100 huts might represent 400-500. 350 years of occupation might represent 10 generations for Meare alone there would be 4,000 to 5,000 burials if burials there were.' Morland continued to write, and doubtless speak, to Bulleid about a suggested early phase of square huts, hurdlework and oak piles preceding the round hut phase at Meare, just as he had for Glastonbury. By 1927 he wrote 'At 90 years of age I have not the sustained vigour to work it out neither would I if I could. I look upon this *history* as the crowning point of *your work* and that you should do it and get the kudos.'

In 1924 there occurred an event that damaged the relationship between Bulleid and Gray. Bulleid wrote a small booklet on *The Lake Villages of Somerset* and it was published by the Glastonbury Antiquarian Society; it was dedicated to John Morland. The booklet was enormously popular and is now in its seventh edition; there is relatively little difference between the first and the seventh, other than a few references to the work at Meare. Gray was annoyed that the booklet appeared under the sole authorship of Bulleid and he refused to sell it in the Somerset Society's premises at Taunton. There is no reference to it in the correspondence between the two, or in any of the excavation notebooks. But from the beginning of their joint excavations there never was much comradeship. In 1939, after 35 years of working together, a letter from Gray to Bulleid begins 'My dear Bulleid'; one might have thought by then that Christian names would have been in use, but on site it was equally formal.

Gray and his wife visited the Bulleids at Dymboro once or twice a year, and 'we as a family disliked these visits; my father and mother were usually a bit on edge' (A G) and personal remarks were often barbed. Bulleid always said he could never have managed the financing of the excavations without Gray's help, but the family was irritated by Gray's egotism. 'For example, for the opening of the Wyndham (archaeological) Gallery, we went to Taunton. I do not think my father was on the platform but Mr Gray was much in evidence and throughout the proceedings my father's name and work was never mentioned' (A G). Mrs Bulleid was a staunch defender of her husband who tended to avoid confrontation with Gray if at all possible.

The excavations at Meare Village West went on until 1932 and continued to draw many visitors to the site. A Visitors' Book was kept and notes the presence of three visitors on day one (May 24th 1910), the regular visits of local societies and others from as far afield as Manchester, Bristol and Bournemouth. The listing of visitors' home towns shows the worldwide interest in Glastonbury town and the excavations. Among the visitors was a young W J Wedlake,

*32. A page from the Meare Village West visitors' book, note Sir Arthur and Lady Conan Doyle and a visitor from Australia*

1925.

Mon., June 8th

Sir Arthur & Lady Conan Doyle

Wed., June 10th

Edward W. Keakes.
Weston-s-Mare.

Wm. McLeavid.

P. V. Oldford, Vicar of Meare, a Mr. Cekford.

R. Slavin

Thursday, June 11th

R. J. Parry, Cheddar

R. Parry, Bishops Castle.

Friday, June 12th

Mrs A Williams - Monmouthshire

A. E. Smith Nottingham.

M. Bunny Nottingham

Margaret Hiller Shearman Philadelphia - USA.

A. R. Brodd Australia.

who was to become a stalwart of the excavation team from 1928 - 1936.

Near the end of the explorations at the West Village, Bulleid went on a field trip with the Society of Antiquaries to Yugoslavia. Mary Flower, daughter of Sir Cyril Flower, wrote an account of the visit to a country that in 1929 was essentially rural and underdeveloped, yet had a minority element very much at the top. By car and coach the party would leave the hotel at 6 am, to negotiate unmade roads and tracks, with frequent punctures and spare tyres festooning the vehicles. Archaeological sites were visited, with local dignitaries clustered around, waiting patiently for the cavalcade to arrive. Generous luncheons, with many speeches, took several hours before the party embarked again for more sightseeing. The evening banquets would end near midnight, with a few hours rest before the 6 am start next day. Bulleid was much in demand, quietly and calmly dispensing external and internal medications; he also managed to make some sketches of the rural farming equipment and the richly-decorated ancient pottery in Yugoslav museums.

Bulleid's talent and experience in drawing is best displayed in his pencil and inked representations of pottery, but also in his patterns for fabrics and wallpaper. He worked on the patterns mostly in the 1920s and 1930s and had intended them to go into some form of production, but the onset of the war prevented the plan from reaching fulfilment. His surviving patterns, often of interlaced leaves and twigs, were probably inspired by the Celtic designs he had uncovered at the Lake Villages.

By 1932 a considerable part of the Meare Village West had been explored (at a cost of £1305-15-10), and Bulleid and Gray considered that sufficient had been done to gain an understanding of the site. The work of drawing plans and sections, and the cataloguing of the enormous number of finds, had been undertaken by both men during the years and the monographs were in preparation. Bulleid was 70 and Gray 60 - surely a good time to call excavations to a halt. Bulleid seems to have taken on a new lease of life at this time. He was eager to start work at Meare Village East, but he also planned a visit, with Annie, to Australia, and he got involved in new discoveries made by peat-cutters just south of the Meare 'island'.

In June 1933 peat cutters at the Eclipse Peat Works cut through a wooden trackway on Meare Heath. News of the discovery reached John Morland who passed on the details to Bulleid in a letter dated 18 July 1933:

'I saw Councillor Alexander (manager of the peat works) last night ... He tells me that in digging say 8 ft down in the peat, they have come down on a trackway formed of oak making as he says a kind of tramway ... He thinks the direction of the piece of way exposed would be in a direct line from Meare to the Manor House at Shapwick. You will want to see it and I told Alexander I should write to you.'

Bulleid had already seen evidence for this trackway in about 1890 when searching the area for lake settlements but the remains of worked timber were not followed up. Mr Alexander willingly gave permission for Bulleid to undertake fieldwork and on several occasions during 1933 he examined, recorded and photographed exposures of the Meare Heath trackway. Unfortunately peat cutting had destroyed all but the edge of the track which led to an incorrect interpretation of the structure of the track.

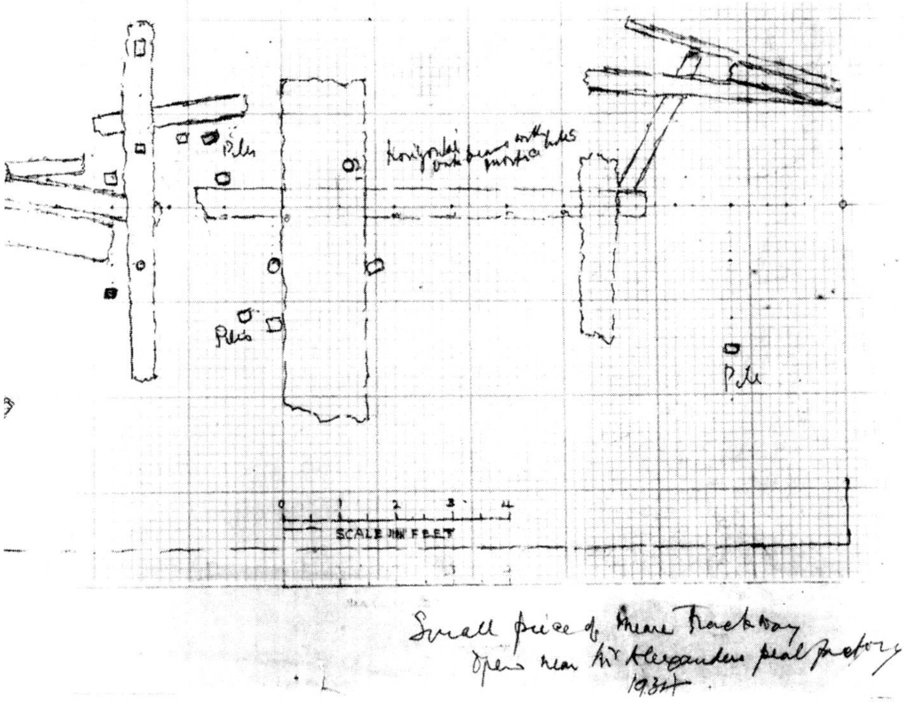


33. *Plan of the Meare Heath track as revealed in 1934*

Bulleid was aware that questions remained unanswered, notably about the width of the trackway, and hoped that in the near future the opportunity would occur to examine a less damaged section. Nothing further was published but in 1934 he found and excavated another length of the trackway in a better state of preservation; this would have allowed him to propose an interpretation more in line with current thoughts which are based on large-scale work in the years 1975-1985. The track consisted of a substructure of brushwood and long timbers laid longitudinally; upon this heavy beams were placed transversly to form the walking surface. In the days before dendrochronology and radiocarbon dating, the dating of a feature such as this with no associated artefacts posed a problem. Bulleid pursued the only line open to him and reviewed all archaeological discoveries made in the area and the depth at which they were found where this was known. This led him to the conclusion that the trackway was probably Bronze Age. Radiocarbon dating has now confirmed this giving a construction date of about 1400 B.C. for this one and a quarter mile long walkway built on raised bog.

Bulleid was called to the peat-workings again in 1936-38, to record and recover three hoards of silver and bronze coins buried with pewter vessels in the 4th century A.D. in the parish of Shapwick. His rapid attendance ensured that the finds were secured for the British Museum and the Somerset County Museum through the laws of Treasure Trove.

In the winter of 1933-34 Bulleid and Annie, along with their daughters Armynell and Christine, went to Australia to see the Austin families. Bulleid lost no opportunity to visit sites and collect artefacts. He kept a diary which contains brief records of his visits to aboriginal sites:

> *3 January:* 'Greenvale (Victoria). Geoff and I dug into a 'Black Man's Oven' did not find anything'
> *4 January:* 'Greenvale. Walked along shore, inspected black camps and picked up several implements. Wonderful site for things on either side of exit creek for 1/4 mile or so'.
> *5 January:* 'Greenvale. Annie and I had a walk along the river after tea. Annie found an unfinished Blackman's axe and I a rubbing stone'.
> *6 January:* 'Greenvale. Walked with Annie to blackman's camping ground near the river'.

34. *James Crane photographed by Bulleid with the hoard of late Roman silver coins and pewter vessels that he found whilst peat digging at Shapwick in 1936*

*17 February:* 'Dymboro (Victoria). Motored ... to Mount William in the Black Mountains... Visited black fellows work shops of Diorite stone - outcrop on hill top'. (This outing clearly had its problems) 'Stupid chauffeur, arrived home very late. Interesting day, very if it had not been for the stupidity of the driver'.
*31 March:* (On the return sailing they stopped at Cairo.) '...visited the museum and saw the objects from Tutankamen's tomb and other things. Very wonderful and beautiful... Bought scarab. Motored through the bazaars and then 9 miles to the pyramids of Gaza'.

The scarab was bought from a dealer in Shepherd's Hotel in Cairo who tried to hassle Bulleid into an expensive purchase. Bulleid took his time, examined each scarab with his magnifying glass, and finally bought a small less-expensive scarab. The dealer said 'Thank you very much, you know too much'.

He returned to Somerset to become involved in a major dispute within the Glastonbury Antiquarian Society. By 1934 both he and Gray were worried about the state of the Lake Village finds in Glastonbury Museum and they proposed the removal of the material to Taunton. Although Horne and Morland were in support, the local vicar of St. John's Church, Glastonbury, mounted a campaign to prevent the move taking place. His strategy was to tackle the issue both within the committee room and publicly in the local press. At the 1934 Glastonbury Antiquarian Society Annual General Meeting, the vicar proposed Major Bath as president in opposition to the re-election of Horne. The vicar made it quite plain that his move was 'a vote censure on the Committee and everyone who had to do with the removal of the Museum exhibits to Taunton'. Stephen Morland proposed the re-election of Horne. Both candidates left the room and the ensuing vote of 14 to 9 resulted in Horne being returned. Nevertheless opposition to the transfer of the collection was such that the idea was dropped. The more important material from the Lake Village was taken to Taunton for reasons of safety in 1940 and was placed in Cell 15 in the Territorial Hall for the duration of the war. In 1945 a further attempt to permanently transfer the whole collection to Taunton was again vetoed.

In 1934 31 members of the Antiquarian Society visited the excavations then taking place at Maiden Castle, Dorset. The party, which included Arthur Bulleid, was taken around the site by Colonel Drew FSA. William Wedlake who was employed on the site wrote to Horne on 18 October 1934 'I hope Dr. Bulleid enjoyed his visit here, it was a pity Dr. Wheeler wasn't here as he particularly wanted to meet Dr. Bulleid'. Bulleid paid a second visit to the excavations in 1935 as revealed in a letter written by Tessa Wheeler to Horne on 30 September of that year. 'It was a real privilege to meet Dr. Bulleid. I have almost grown up (archaeologically) with his work and he himself has been something of a legend. I think I would be liking him awfully much. He looks at one steadily.' This is high praise indeed from someone involved in one of the most advanced excavations of the time and gives an insight into the esteem in which Bulleid was held.

Bulleid's interests included geology. In 1943 he published a biography of Thomas Hawkins (1810-1889). Hawkins, who spent much of the first half of his life in the Glastonbury area, was a major fossil collector. His collection, particularly notable for the ichthyosaurs and plesiosaurs found in quarrying at Street, was purchased by the British Museum.

Bulleid's most important geological research and publication was on the Burtle beds of the Somerset Levels. Islands of sand and gravel, they are found in the lower valleys of the rivers Parrett, Brue and Tone. Research had been initiated by Dr. C Balfour Steward and Mr W Ussher prior to the First World War. On the departure of the former to Switzerland he passed his papers to Bulleid in the hope that he would continue the work. This he did in association with Dr. Wilfrid Jackson of Manchester Museum. They plotted the occurrences of the Burtle beds and recorded their composition. In all 27 Burtle beds were traced. Some such as Greylake, Middlezoy, and Aller were being quarried for their gravel enabling Bulleid and Jackson to draw and photograph sections and to retrieve faunal and molluscan material. Armynell Goodall has already noted the unusual method of taking preliminary samples from the unstable sand sections. Bulleid and Jackson reported their results in 1936 and 1941. Their conclusion was that the Burtle beds were marine in origin and that they formed in an interglacial period. In 1971 these conclusions were disputed and a glacial origin for the deposits postulated. However, further research substantiated Bulleid and Jackson and their published work on the Burtle beds remains crucial for anyone undertaking research on the subject.

## Excavations at Meare Village East 1933-38

In 1933, Bulleid and Gray started new excavations at Meare Village East; work here went on to 1938 when war stopped proceedings. After the war Gray alone continued until 1956 when he finally gave up, aged 84.

The excavation method at both of the Meare sites remained unchanged throughout the period 1910-1956: raps were dug, finds removed, sections noted and plans drawn where structures were seen. A digging house, three-roomed, was built for the Meare work in 1910 and carefully maintained and repaired year by year. It survived on the East site until 1989 when it was removed for safe-keeping and re-erection as part of the local displays of archaeology in the Levels. It was found to contain equipment used by Bulleid and Gray, finds from Gray's last season, and newspapers (for wrapping finds) dating back to the years 1890-1955. Also surviving are one or two of the paper knives (letter openers) made from oak found in the Meare excavations. Funds were often short and the sale of these between 1932 and 1949 yielded £71-2-1, with a small part realised through the sale of slingstones. The knives were made locally, some by Bulleid himself in 1933. The total cost of manufacture was £19-1-6.

Visitors to the East excavations were numerous as usual. One fine day in September 1936 there were 20 visitors: 8 from Somerset, 3 from Dorset, 1 from Essex, 4 from South Africa and 4 from South India. The next day, visitors came from a Pembrokeshire vicarage and Downside Abbey, and a party from a Women's Institute also arrived. Bulleid's last excavation season began on August 22 1938; his notebook describes the day. 'Began work with six men at the south edge of mound XXIV, which was exposed during the digging of 1936. Rain stopped play'.

W. J. Wedlake worked for Bulleid and Gray during the last years at Meare West and the early years at Meare East. His own recollections of the excavations are as colourful as was he himself. He was not a local peat-digger or farm labourer and found the work of cutting raps very hard, unlike the locals who could dig all day fortified by scrumpy. When visitors came, Bulleid tended to keep out of the way, preferring to get on with the drawing or recording, while Gray would try to impress the visitors with the finds and thereby encourage them to donate something to the excavation fund. Wedlake recalls that visitors from America were often amusing in their ignorance of the site; they would often ask 'Well tell me where is this so-called Village?', to which Bulleid if present would say with a slight chuckle 'You're standing on it'. One day, while rummaging in the box of finds, a lady picked up a long cylindrical object and took it to Bulleid. 'What is this supposed to be?', she said. He replied very seriously 'Excreta of a goat'. 'What on earth is that?'she asked. 'Goat dropping', Bulleid said, subduing a laugh, whereupon she did just that.

Wedlake recalls visits by the Bulleid family to the exca-

35. *John Masefield (poet laureate), Ethelbert Horne, Arthur Bulleid and Harold St George Gray at Meare Village East on 9 September1935*

vations, and how one of the boys (Humfrey) would sometimes hide behind a spoil heap with his catapult. When Parsons the foreman, a very large-bottomed man, bent over to pick up a find, young Humfrey would launch a missile; the response from Parsons is unprintable. Bulleid was apparently a leader who inspired confidence in his small team; certainly by the 1930s he was a senior figure greatly respected by all who encountered him. Harry Godwin, then developing environmental work in the Levels, was impressed by his ability to grasp the implications of the newly-developing science of pollen analysis and macrofossil studies, and wrote in his book on *The Archives of the Peat Bogs* 'I have always counted it as one of the major benefits and pleasures of the Somerset investigations that they brought me into contact with so distinguished and lovable a man.'

36. *Mound 15B at Meare Village East in 1935*

The problems of publication for the Meare sites were very great and it says much for both Bulleid and Gray that they managed to complete the texts and most of the drawings of the Meare West report in the years 1930-1950 when they were quite old. And here family circumstances must have played a part in the delays in publication. Bulleid retired from his medical practice just before the 1939-1945 war, and must have planned to work on both Meare reports. His son Hilary was to take on the practice, but he joined the Armed Forces, and his father had to keep the practice going in Midsomer Norton. By 1945, Bulleid was 83 years old and had lost six precious years of full-time work on the Meare sites. Meare Village West appeared in three volumes, in 1948, 1953 and 1966; Meare Village East had to be written up from notebooks, photographs and finds, and appeared only in 1987.

## The Meare Lake Villages

What was and is missing from their records, particularly from Bulleid's notebooks, is his interpretation of the sites at Meare. They were considered at first to be yet more Glastonbury-type settlements, but Bulleid soon recognised that they were different from the classic Lake Village. At Meare the occupation took place directly upon the dried surface of a raised bog, and not within a swamp. No crannog-type substructure, of stones, clay and wood, was necessary to firm-up the base upon which the occupation was to occur. Again, there were many rectangular settings of beams and other timbers set in place in the first phase of construction. Again, some seemed random, as if dumped, but others were firmly in place. But overall this low timber was sparse, particularly at Meare East, when compared with Glastonbury. Much of the occupied surfaces at the Meare sites consisted of spreads of the clay dumped upon the natural peat surface, with hearths built upon the clay floors, and renewals gradually building up the deposits as they gently subsided into the peat through regular, perhaps annual, floods. Bulleid thought there were some round huts at Meare, marked by rings of stakes, but he was puzzled at their relative scarcity and he interpreted some of the stake rings as the remnants of tents rather than wattle and daub houses. Other areas of stakes may have held windbreak hurdles. The occupations at Meare were probably mostly open-air, centred around substantial hearths.

One of the reasons why Bulleid and Gray were encouraged to dig on these sites was because their preliminary soundings had yielded so much material. Large quantities of animal bone, barrow-loads of grain, boxes of pottery, and a wide range of personal and industrial equipment were eventually recovered, and Gray in particular was satisfied with the yield for the Somerset County Museum of which he was Curator (1901-1949). Many glass beads, whole necklaces sometimes, bronze brooches and armlets, bone and antler combs, iron tools, spindle whorls and loom-weights, and many other objects were recovered, as well as unfinished artefacts. The current interpretation of these sites at Meare is that they represent a seasonal market or fair, held on common ground otherwise of little economic use to the Iron Age communities living at Glastonbury and on the uplands around the Levels. Here, on a desolate peatbog, were gathered each year different groups of people, who camped, feasted, made and traded goods of great variety, talked and perhaps established partnerships both personal and community-based. After a week or so, the various groups dispersed back to their homes and the winter floods soon once again overran the meeting-place. The clay spreads were washed by water, and required renewing and reshaping each year. For several centuries, from about 150 B.C. to about 100 A.D., Meare functioned as the social centre for Iron Age societies, but with the onset of more serious flooding, water-laid clays began to be laid down and the site was abandoned forever. This scenario is not one that Bulleid and Gray proposed, but Bulleid had provided hints of seasonality in those thoughts that he put into paper, and he had identified the unusual environmental circumstances of the Meare occupations.

37. *Bulleid at Glastonbury Lake Village*

## Final Words

Arthur Bulleid died at his home, Dymboro, Midsomer Norton on December 27 1951; he was 89. Although there had been various earlier archaeological excavations in the Somerset Levels, on the Abbot's Way for example, Bulleid was the pioneer *par excellence*, discovering, identifying, exploring and then publishing the report on the total examination of an Iron Age settlement - the Glastonbury Lake Village. This site, found in 1892, remains the basis upon which all other British Iron Age settlements are compared and judged. A number of research dissertations have been founded on the site and its material remains, numerous articles have appeared in both the learned and popular press, as well as various books, reconstruction models, drawings and full size copies, and the life of 'the Celtic Warrior in his watery fortress' is never far from writings on life in the past. Bulleid would certainly appreciate the profound interest inspired by his work, and would chuckle if he could read some of the fanciful rubbish created over the years.

In view of all that had gone before, the final words should be Harold St. George Gray's, in his obituary notice of Arthur Bulleid:

> 'he was a most careful, accurate and painstaking observer, and exceedingly pleasant to work with... Bulleid was never happier than when working at the Lake Villages where he made many friends who appreciated his archaeological enthusiasm... The writer of these notes, who spent many weeks of his life... under Dr. Bulleid's roof, always found him kind and friendly, and of a decidedly hospitable nature'.

# Bibliography of Arthur Bulleid


Bulleid, A 1892.
Ancient Canoe found near Glastonbury, *Somerset and Dorset Notes and Queries* 3, number 20, 121
Bulleid, A 1892.
British Village, Glastonbury, *Somerset and Dorset Notes and Queries* 3, number 20, 122 - 125
Bulleid, A 1894.
The Lake Village near Glastonbury, *PSANHS* 40, 141 - 151
Bulleid, A and Gray, H St G 1904.
The Glastonbury Lake Village, *PSANHS* 50, 68 - 93
Bulleid, A 1904.
Romano-British remains found at Killings Knap Quarry, *Downside Review* 23, number 69, 305- 311
Bulleid, A and Gray, H St G 1905.
The Glastonbury Lake Village, *PSANHS* 51, 77 - 104
Bulleid, A 1906.
Prehistoric boat, found at Shapwick, 1906, *PSANHS* 52, 51 - 54
Bulleid, A and Gray, H St G 1906.
The Glastonbury Lake Village, *PSANHS* 52, 94 - 129
Bulleid, A and Gray, H St G 1907.
The Glastonbury Lake Village, *PSANHS* 53, 101 - 147
Bulleid, A 1908.
Meare Lake Village, *PSANHS* 54 Part 1, 40 - 42
Bulleid, A and Gray, H St G 1910.
Meare Lake Village, *PSANHS* 56 Part 1, 38 - 43
Bulleid, A 1911.
The Murtry Hill Stones, *PSANHS* 57 Part 1, 36 - 38
Bulleid, A and Gray, H St G 1911.
*The Glastonbury Lake Village* Volume I
Bulleid, A and Gray, H St G 1911.
Meare Lake Village, *PSANHS* 57 Part 1, 42 - 47
Bulleid A and Gray, H St G 1912.
Meare Lake Village, *PSANHS* 58 Part 1, 38 - 41
Bulleid, A 1913 - 1914.
Romano-British Potteries in Mid-Somerset, *Proc Soc Ant* 26, 137 - 144
Bulleid, A and Gray, H St G 1917.
*The Glastonbury Lake Village* Volume II
Bulleid, A 1924.
*The Lake Villages of Somerset*
Bulleid, A 1924.
Field Names in the Parish of Paulton, *Somerset and Dorset Notes and Queries*, March 1924, Volume 18, 9
Bulleid, A 1924.
Field Names in the Parish of Midsomer Norton, *Somerset and Dorset Notes and Queries* June 1924, Volume 18, 26 - 27
Bulleid, A and Horne, E 1924 - 5.
The Roman House at Keynsham, Somerset, *Archaeologia* 75, 109-138
Bulleid, A 1925.

Prehistoric man around Bath, *The Book of Bath*, 11-19
Bulleid, A 1926.
The Mound, Glastonbury, *PSANHS* 72, 52 - 54
Bulleid, A and Gray, H St G 1926.
Meare Lake Village Excavations, *PSANHS* 72 Part 1, 37 - 40
Bulleid, A 1927.
Kilmersdon Road Quarry, Radstock, *PSANHS* 73, 132
Bulleid, A 1929.
Bronze Palstave, Peasedown St John, *PSANHS* 75, 98
Bulleid, A and Gray, H St G 1932.
The Meare Lake Village Excavations 1932, *PSANHS* 78, 126 - 127
Bulleid, A 1933.
Ancient Trackway in Meare Heath, *PSANHS* 79, 19 - 29
Bulleid, A and Gray, H St G 1933.
The Meare Lake Village Excavations 1933, *PSANHS* 79, 112 - 113
Bulleid, A and Gray, H St G 1934.
The Meare Lake Village Excavations 1934, *PSANHS* 80, 68 - 69
Bulleid, A and Gray, H St G 1935.
The Meare Lake Village Excavations 1935, *PSANHS* 81, 256 - 258
Bulleid, A 1936.
Somerset Lake Village, *Bristol Medico-Chirurgical Journal* 53, 187-218
Bulleid, A and Gray, H St G 1936.
The Meare Lake Village Excavations 1936, *PSANHS* 82, 236 - 237
Bulleid, A and Jackson, J W 1937.
The Burtle Sand Beds of Somerset, *PSANHS* 83, 171 - 195
Bulleid, A and Gray, H St G 1937.
The Meare Lake Village Excavations 1937, *PSANHS* 83, 209 - 211
Bulleid, A and Gray, H St G 1938.
The Meare Lake Village Excavations 1938, *PSANHS* 84, 169 - 171
Bulleid, A 1941.
Notes on Some Chambered Long Barrows of North Somerset, *PSANHS* 87, 56 - 71
Bulleid, A and Jackson J W 1941.
The Burtle Sand Beds of Somerset, *PSANHS* 87, 111 - 116
Bulleid, A 1943.
Notes on the Life and Work of Thomas Hawkins, *PSANHS* 89, 59 - 71
Bulleid, A 1945.
Oak Piles in Kings Sedgemoor, *PSANHS* 91, 109
Bulleid, A and Gray H St G 1948.
*The Meare Lake Village* Volume I
Gray, H St G and Bulleid, A 1953.
*The Meare Lake Village* Volume II

*PSANHS*: Proceedings of the Somerset Archaeological and Natural History Society

*38. Bulleid's sketch of a heron eating a frog*